ENCOUNTER

experiencing God in the everyday

mark hart

**Leader's Guide**

ASCENSION PRESS

West Chester, Pennsylvania

*Nihil obstat:*     Reverend Robert A. Pesarchick, S.T.D.
                    *Censor Librorum*
                    January 3, 2013

*Imprimatur:*      +Most Reverend Charles J. Chaput, O.F.M. CAP.
                    Archbishop of Philadelphia
                    January 24, 2013

*Encounter* is a resource of *The Great Adventure* Catholic Bible Study Program.

Jeff Cavins, General Editor, *The Great Adventure,* and creator of the *Bible Timeline* Learning System.

Sarah Christmyer, Editor, *The Great Adventure.*

Mark Hart, Author and Presenter, *Encounter: Experiencing God in the Everyday.*

Unless otherwise noted, Scripture passages have been taken from the *Revised Standard Version–Catholic Edition.* Copyright © 1946, 1952, 1971 by the Division of Christian Education of the National Council of the Churches of Christ in the United States of America. All rights reserved.

Map of "The Divided Kingdom" from *The Great Adventure Bible Timeline* by Jeff Cavins and Sarah Christmyer. Copyright © 2004 Ascension Press. All rights reserved.

"Examination of Conscience" (page 37) and "Brain Teasers" (page 47) adapted from *Edge Youth Ministry.* Copyright © 2012 Life Teen, Inc. Used with permission.

Ascension Press
Post Office Box 1990
West Chester, PA 19380
Orders: 1-800-376-0520
AscensionPress.com
BibleStudyforCatholics.com

Cover Design: Devin Schadt

Printed in the United States of America

ISBN: 978-1-935940-49-4

# TABLE OF CONTENTS

# Welcome

Several years ago, I felt the Lord put an uncomfortable burden on my heart. I had been working with high-school and college youth for more than ten years. I knew their culture, their struggles, and their issues. But then the Lord called me out of my comfort zone.

I had little desire to interact with middle-school students. They constantly digressed in their conversations. They were hyper and giggly and would grow a foot between the time a class began and ended. I wanted to go to the middle-school world about as much as Jonah wanted to go to Nineveh, and I let God know it. Of course, God met me in my stubbornness and made it clear through my prayer that the "Ninevites"—I mean middle schoolers—needed to know his love, too. Before I could jump ship, like Jonah, I found myself volunteering to lead Bible study with the middle-school students. My life has never been the same.

Once I got over my initial fears, annoyances, and preconceived notions, I discovered the most amazing thing about these students: They are so open! Not yet jaded by life, these young souls are thirsting for direction, affirmation, and purpose.

Some say that this age group is too shallow and "squirmy" to study Scripture or to pray deeply. I disagree. Leading young teens into God's truth may be a challenge, but with the right tools for planting the seed of the Word, and with a solid strategy for tilling the topsoil of their hearts, you will see that Word take root and begin to bear fruit in their lives.

Don't worry if you aren't sure you have what it takes. The most important thing to remember is to be *authentic*. You don't have to have all the answers. You don't have to be the hippest parent or the coolest teacher. *What these young souls need more than anything is your attention and love*. The best way to get them to care about Scripture is to care about *them*. In every group discussion and activity, be interested in what they have to say, and affirm them for sharing. Your students will continue to rise to the occasion.

Christ's challenge to the disciples to "follow" him (Matthew 4:19) was more than an invitation to a new vocation; it was the highest validation of their worth. In *Encounter*, you are introducing these young souls to their Savior in an intimate new way. You are offering them more than answers to their adolescent moral dilemmas; you are offering them renewed purpose for their lives. In the sessions that follow, they will "encounter" the living God in comforting yet surprising new ways. Throughout the study, they will be given invitations—some obvious and some subtle—to follow Jesus in their daily lives. Along the way, you as a leader will be reminded of your great worth in the eyes of God, not only in how you shepherd young souls but in how you are loved as a daughter or son of God.

Thank you for entering into this journey with your young people. Our hope is that you will (all) be immeasurably blessed by it.

Now, let's have some fun.

Mark Hart

# Part One
## INTRODUCTION TO *ENCOUNTER*: EXPERIENCING GOD IN THE EVERYDAY

## ABOUT *ENCOUNTER*

*Encounter* is an eight-part, video-based introduction to Scripture that leads middle-school students into a life-changing encounter with God. This fast-paced and dynamic journey through the Bible is based on the popular *Great Adventure Bible Timeline* by Jeff Cavins and can be used in the classroom, for youth-group or home-school catechesis, or as a family Bible study.

In eight, half-hour video sessions, Mark Hart invites young people to get to know God and his deep love for each of them. He introduces them to the great biblical heroes of the Faith and helps them find echoes of (and help for!) their own daily struggles and concerns. In the process, they will become familiar with the basic outline of salvation history and God's plan for their lives.

## MATERIALS

To lead *Encounter* in your classroom, youth group, or home, you will need one set of *Encounter* DVDs, this Leader's Guide, and one Student Workbook for each child in the program (described below). The *Encounter* Review Pack contains a complete set of these components and can be ordered risk-free while you evaluate the program:

- **Leader's Guide:** The Leader's Guide contains all the information you will need to plan and lead each of the eight sessions in this study. Student Workbook pages have been reduced and reprinted in this Leader's Guide with "wrap-around" notes and tips to guide you as you prepare for class. General instructions and helpful notes and resources are included at the front and back of this guide. For additional resources, including free downloads to help with promoting your *Encounter* study, go to BibleStudyforCatholics.com.

- ***Encounter* DVDs:** Teaching by Mark Hart is provided in eight, 30-minute DVD presentations designed to work together with the Student Workbook. Although it is helpful to be familiar with the *Bible Timeline* prior to leading this class, these DVDs make it easy to simply plug-and-play, so you can learn about the *Bible Timeline* right along with your students!

- **Student Workbook:** Each session in the Student Workbook includes an introduction, pages to complete while watching the DVD, and take-home activities and resources for reinforcing the sessions at home.

Everyone participating in *Encounter* should have a Catholic Bible.

Additional *Bible Timeline* resources and teacher's aids (promotional materials as well as *Bible Timeline* charts, bookmarks, maps, playing cards, and so on) are available online at BibleStudyforCatholics.com.

## PROGRAM OUTLINE

*Encounter* is a fun, interactive presentation of *The Great Adventure Bible Timeline* that introduces middle-school kids to the Bible and helps them see its value for their lives. They will emerge from the study knowing the general flow of the biblical story and with a basic understanding of the major time periods and events of the Bible. But the primary emphasis is on fostering an "encounter" with God and with the heroes of the Faith they read about in the Bible, as well as whetting their appetites for reading and learning more.

*Encounter* recognizes the challenges that are unique to teaching children of middle-school age, including their wide range of maturity levels and the need to keep them on track. It is designed to help you—the teacher or parent—to reach them effectively in a way that speaks directly to their lives.

*Encounter* is divided into segments, each approximately thirty minutes in length. Each DVD contains two sessions:

**DISC ONE:**

- Session One: An Introduction to the Bible
- Session Two: Early World (Genesis 1–11)

**DISC TWO:**

- Session Three: Patriarchs – Egypt & Exodus (Part 1, Genesis 12–50)
- Session Four: Egypt & Exodus (Part 2) – Desert Wanderings – Conquest & Judges (Exodus, Numbers, Joshua, and Judges)

**DISC THREE:**

- Session Five: Royal Kingdom – Divided Kingdom (1&2 Samuel; 1&2 Kings)
- Session Six: Exile – Return – Maccabean Revolt (2 Kings, Ezra, Nehemiah, and 1 Maccabees)

**DISC FOUR:**

- Session Seven: Messianic Fulfillment (Gospel of Luke)
- Session Eight: The Church (Acts of the Apostles)

# FREQUENTLY ASKED QUESTIONS (FAQS)

## Who can lead *Encounter?*

This resource is designed for youth ministers, teachers, DREs, catechists, and parents who want to present the Bible to their middle-school students but have little time to develop study programs from scratch.

## How long does the program take?

*Encounter* is an eight-part program that can be offered in eight consecutive meetings, in four longer sessions, or in a shorter time frame, depending on the needs of your parish. To get the full value of the program, all eight sessions should be shown, and they should be shown in order, as each builds upon the last. Here are three popular options:

- **Eight weeks**

  Most middle-school groups schedule eight consecutive meetings as a stand-alone program or at the start of a larger semester on Sacred Scripture.

- **Four weeks**

  Some groups find that an eight-week commitment is difficult to make within their calendar, and instead choose to double up the sessions and offer them over a one-month period.

- **Full day or weekend**

  Still others use *Encounter* as part of a weekend retreat experience, or as a full-day seminar or overnight "lock-in." It's really up to you!

If you have questions about how to best implement this study into your formation program, our Study Consultants are ready to help you. Just call 1-800-376-0520.

## What types of middle-school groups use *Encounter?*

*Encounter* is a good choice for any middle-school group study. It can be used effectively in a school or religious education classroom, with home-school groups, as a youth-group Bible study, or as family Bible study. Many middle-school groups have invited parents to the meetings, as well, offering an intergenerational time for families to grow together in knowledge and community. The same timeline period breakdown is followed in all of the eight-part *Bible Timeline* programs, making it ideal for whole-family catechesis within the parish.

In Part Two of this Leader's Guide, specific tips are offered for optimizing the effectiveness of the *Encounter* program for your particular group.

## How does *Encounter* fit into *The Great Adventure: A Journey Through the Bible?*

*The Great Adventure* Catholic Bible study program provides a simple approach to Scripture study that is based on first getting the "big picture" of the underlying biblical story. *The Great Adventure's* unique, color-coded *Bible Timeline* learning system, developed by Jeff Cavins, breaks the narrative down into easily remembered time periods and then walks people through the story as it unfolds in just fourteen books of the Bible. The remaining books of the Bible are read in light of that overall context and in light of Catholic teaching.

There are *Bible Timeline* programs and resources for all ages. For adults, these programs include a one-day seminar; an eight-part *Quick Journey Through the Bible*; a *Bible Timeline Guided Journal*; and a twenty-four part *Bible Timeline* study. For younger age groups, the *Bible Timeline* offers *T3: The*

*Teen Timeline*[1] for high-school students; *The Great Adventure Kids* materials for children; and, now, *Encounter,* aimed at kids in middle school.

*Encounter* is designed specifically with the preteen (or young teen) demographic in mind. You will notice that several points, people, and stories found in *The Great Adventure* adult studies have been glossed over or even omitted entirely. Conversely, you will find that other stories and teaching points are covered in great detail in *Encounter*. In no way is this meant to imply that the omitted points are unimportant or that those covered in greater detail here are more important. Decisions on content were made to ensure that middle-school students would be given the most fundamental points in broad-stroke form, while ensuring that *Encounter* studies maintain a faster-paced, engaging, and culturally appropriate approach that keeps students' attention.

### Do I need to be familiar with *The Bible Timeline* to lead *Encounter?*

An understanding of the *Bible Timeline* will enrich the discussions you can have with students about the program and may help you answer questions that come up outside of class, but it is not required. For more information: BibleStudyforCatholics.com or AscensionPress.com.

### What are the *Bible Timeline* periods and colors?

The *Bible Timeline* learning system is based on a simple, color-coded timeline of Bible history. It breaks the entire biblical narrative down into twelve easily remembered time periods and then follows the story as it unfolds in fourteen historical, or "narrative," books of the Bible, from Genesis to the Acts of the Apostles. The remaining books of the Bible are then read in light of that overall context and in light of Catholic teaching.

Each period of the *Bible Timeline* is assigned a unique color as a memory aid. For example, the color turquoise is used for the period of the Early World, during which the world was created, because it represents the color of the earth seen from space.

Here's a list of the time periods and colors used to remember them, along with the books of the Bible that provide the basic narrative:

| *Bible Timeline* Period | Narrative Book(s) | Color | Color Meaning |
| --- | --- | --- | --- |
| Early World | Genesis 1–11 | Turquoise | The color of the earth viewed from space |
| Patriarchs | Genesis 12–50 | Burgundy | God's blood covenant with Abraham |
| Egypt & Exodus | Exodus | Red | The Red Sea |
| Desert Wanderings | Numbers | Tan | The color of the desert |
| Conquest & Judges | Joshua, Judges | Green | The green hills of Canaan |
| Royal Kingdom | 1 & 2 Samuel, 1 Kings 1–11 | Purple | Royalty |
| Divided Kingdom | 1 Kings 12–22, 2 Kings | Black | Israel's darkest period |
| Exile | 2 Kings | Baby blue | Judah "singing the blues" in Baby-lon |
| Return | Ezra, Nehemiah | Yellow | Judah returning home to brighter days |
| Maccabean Revolt | 1 Maccabees | Orange | Fire in the oil lamps in the purified Temple |
| Messianic Fulfillment | Luke | Gold | Gifts of the Magi |
| The Church | Acts | White | The spotless bride of Christ |

---

[1] *T3: The Teen Timeline* follows the basic outline of the adult *Quick Journey Through the Bible,* but is made simpler and told in a way that is appealing to teenagers. Participants receive the same full-color, foldout chart and learn much of the same information (while take-home messages are aimed at their age group).

# Part Two
## PREPARING TO LEAD *ENCOUNTER*

## PLANNING AND PROMOTING YOUR STUDY

**Four to eight weeks before the first session:**

- Familiarize yourself with the contents of your Review Pack and read through the Leader's Guide.

- Before the first session, we recommend that you watch all eight DVD presentations (four hours total), following along in the Workbook and Leader's Guide in order to familiarize yourself with the material that will be covered.

- Set the session agenda based on your class needs and time available. Plan for at least 60 minutes. For example:

  » Welcome (10 minutes)

  » DVD Presentation (30-35 minutes)

  » Discussion (10-15 minutes)

  » Closing (5 minutes)

- Arrange for the space and audiovisual equipment you will need.

- If you have more than eight to ten students, consider arranging for one or more volunteers to help facilitate the discussion groups.

- Plan promotion and registration details.

- Begin promoting the study. Free downloadable posters, flyers, and other promotional aids are available at BibleStudyforCatholics.com.

**Two to three weeks before the first session:**

- Order materials: one Student Workbook per middle schooler and extra Leader's Guides for co-leaders (if desired). Be sure to order extra workbooks to account for walk-ins, as students will need to use them the first day. Allow two weeks for shipping. (You may return unused workbooks later for full credit.)

- Invite your co-leaders and volunteer facilitators to review the DVD for the first session with you and prepare for the first meeting and group discussion.

**One to two days before each session:**

- Review the session and note the places on the DVD where you may need to prompt students to write in their workbooks.

- Arrange the audiovisual equipment and materials in the learning space. Test the equipment.

- Arrange for snacks for after-meeting socializing.

## USING *ENCOUNTER* IN VARIOUS SETTINGS

The *Encounter* Scripture study for middle-school students has been used in a variety of settings and formats, some of which were described in Part One of this Leader's Guide. Here are a few more ideas about how to adapt the program to meet the needs of your group:

### *Encounter* with a Youth Group or in a Classroom

*Encounter* is a highly effective program that can be used either as a core part of your curriculum or as a supplemental resource. Teachers often search for a way to bring the Bible to their students and keep it alive in their hearts. *Encounter* is so well-suited for the classroom that any teacher can use it.

*Encounter* is an ideal supplement to a religious education or Scripture class when an overview or introduction to Scripture is needed.

The "Talking It Out" questions and "Taking It Home" activities may be used as homework or for classroom conversation. The important thing is to let *Encounter* be a starting point for deeper conversations during your class times. If desired, homework can be added by assigning readings from the Bible to reinforce what students have learned. These can be drawn from the "Key Events" lists provided for teachers in Part Four of this Leader's Guide next to the student pages for each session.

### Home-School Catechesis

*Encounter* and the *T3 Teen Timeline* Bible studies are easily adapted for use in home-school religious formation efforts. They can be used in individual homes, or communities can set up special Bible study nights when the youth gather in different homes and go through the study together. It's important to create a relaxed atmosphere in these moments. It's important, too, that parents first view the series so that they can best implement and refer back to specific teaching moments in their kids' ongoing formation.

### Family Bible Study

*Encounter* is designed as a family-friendly resource that incorporates proven communication principles, storytelling, and humor that make this study appropriate and informative for middle schoolers and their parents alike. The DVDs offer parents useful, practical insights into how to present the Bible—and the entire Catholic Faith—in a way that their middle schoolers will understand and enjoy.

Parents are encouraged to watch the DVDs either before their youth view them or along with their middle schoolers over the course of several nights, stopping along the way to ask their kids what points jumped out at them most, confused them, or changed their perspective of God.

# Part Three
## LEADER'S GUIDELINES

### FEATURES OF THE LEADER'S GUIDE AND STUDENT WORKBOOK

The Student Workbook contains an introductory letter from Mark Hart; eight, four-page sessions; and an appendix called "Continuing Your Journey." This final section contains a number of extras like "Brain Teasers," "Awful Bible Jokes," and puzzles, some of which are also available as downloads.

Each session contains three parts, normally spread over four pages in the Student Workbook: the Welcome/Introduction; the DVD Presentation and Group Discussion (a two-page spread with the *Bible Timeline* across the bottom); and the Session Wrap-Up.

All of the session pages from the Student Workbook are reproduced in Part Four, together with plans and tips for leading the individual sessions.

### GENERAL INSTRUCTIONS FOR LEADING A SESSION OF *ENCOUNTER*

These instructions apply to all eight sessions of *Encounter*. Details specific to each session are in Part Four of this Leader's Guide.

#### A. The Welcome/Introduction (Steps 1-3)

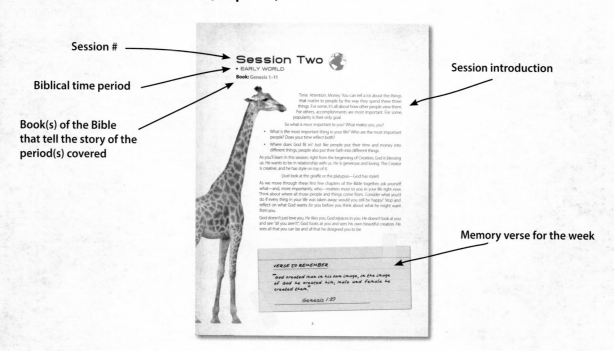

Session #
Biblical time period
Book(s) of the Bible that tell the story of the period(s) covered

Session introduction

Memory verse for the week

 **Step 1** **Welcome**
Welcome students as they arrive and make sure they have their materials.

 **Step 2** **Opening Prayer**
Offer an opening prayer, either the one provided for you or a spontaneous prayer.

**Step 3** **Introduction/ "Verse to Remember"**

In the Student Workbook, each session contains a brief introduction and a "Verse to Remember" feature. To begin, read the introduction aloud.

The verse introduces a theme that will be discussed within the video teaching that week. Ask students to read the verse aloud with you, and tell them what Bible reference (book, chapter, and verse) to write on the appropriate line in their workbooks.

## B. The DVD Presentation and Group Discussion (Steps 4-5)

The main spread of each session in the Student Workbook contains three main elements: the *Bible Timeline* (at the bottom of the page), a list of "Breaking It Down" questions, and a "thumbtacked" sheet of information about each period. All blank lines are for students to fill in as prompted during the DVD presentation. Answers and discussion questions are provided in the Leader's Guide.

**Period information:** to fill out during DVD presentation

**Period color:** For a key to *Bible Timeline* period colors and how to remember them, see page L-4 in this Leader's Guide.

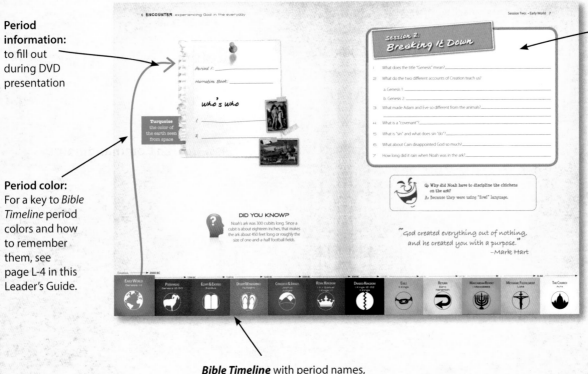

**Breaking It Down:** Mark Hart will talk about (and provide answers to) these questions in his presentation.

*Bible Timeline* with period names, dates, and narrative books

 **Step 4** **Show the DVD – Period Information /Breaking It Down**

The information provided in the Student Workbook is designed to help students retain basic facts and messages from the DVD presentation as follows:

**Period Information:** As Mark Hart explains each *Bible Timeline* period, he will direct the students to fill in lines in the appropriate "thumbtacked" note with the name of the period, the appropriate books of the Bible, and key figures in the narrative (the "Who's Who" part of the sheet). Each note is color coordinated to match the period color as indicated by a colored tab and by the icon at the bottom of the page. A graphic will come up on the video screen while Mark talks, showing the answers. Students may refer to the *Bible Timeline* at the bottom of the page to check their answers or spelling.

The corresponding pages in the Leader's Guide have all answers filled in and feature a list of "Key Events" for each period along with where to find them in the Bible.

**Breaking It Down:** In the Student Workbook, the "Breaking It Down" section contains questions that students should fill in as Mark delivers each presentation. Answers will "pop up" on the screen as he speaks and are filled in for you in this Leader's Guide.

The seven questions selected for each session are by no means the most important, nor are they the only facts to learn about the periods. Rather, these questions are designed to highlight specific fundamentals, foundational story elements, or basics of Catholic teaching. They also help your students to focus on paying attention to the DVD material.

You might encourage them to write down interesting facts, Scripture verses, or questions to bring up during the discussion.

 **Talking It Out**

After the DVD, lead your students in a discussion using the questions provided in this Leader's Guide. These refer back to the storylines and subplots that are discussed in the DVD and help them connect the dots between the stories of salvation history and their own personal stories. Use them to help the students learn to implement the truths they have learned into their daily faith walks in their relationships, homes, schools, and parishes.

Questions can be discussed in a small- or large-group format, depending upon group size and structure.

Before you begin the first discussion group with the kids, review the **Ten Commandments for Good Group Discussions.**

(A free download of this list is available at BibleStudyforCatholics.com.)

## THE TEN COMMANDMENTS FOR GOOD GROUP DISCUSSIONS:

I. Work to build trust and intimacy within your group.

II. Get to the heart of the passage; don't simply skim the surface.

III. Give everyone in your group a chance to talk.

IV. When you share, try to connect your thoughts to the previous speaker. (Build bridges.)

V. When someone is speaking, everyone else is listening.

VI. Never ridicule or cut down another's answers.

VII. When you disagree, do so with respect and charity.

VIII. Do not fear silence.

IX. If you have not completed your homework, allow others the opportunity to express their answers before you respond.

X. Enjoy yourself!

Don't worry about getting through all the questions—and feel free to add questions of your own. Be willing to stay on any question that elicits a strong reaction. Get the students talking and try to be more of a "facilitator" than a "lecturer" during this time. Don't be afraid of silence. Just keep encouraging them to share and wait until one or two do. Be aware of digression, and do your best to keep your students on topic.

## C. The Session Wrap-Up (Steps 6-7)

 ### Taking It Home/Activity Page

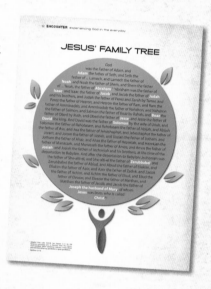

The final page of each session in the Student Workbook is an activity for further reflection or action. Some are referred to in the DVDs and others are not. An explanation or instructions are included with each in Part Four of this Leader's Guide. You may use this activity to fill in extra class time or encourage your students to read through it on their own at home.

**Before closing, review the "Verse to Remember."** If time permits, discuss it for a few minutes, asking the students what they take from it and how it relates to their daily lives, now that they have heard Mark's talk.

OPTIONAL: Encourage students to memorize the "Verse to Remember," and offer a small snack or prize the following week to those who do. Depending on your instructional goals and the time available, consider asking them to read through the stories covered in each session on their own time, bringing any questions they have to your next meeting. These readings are listed in the margins of each session under the heading "Key Events."

Challenge your youth to share what they have learned with their parents and siblings and even to quiz their family members so that they may all learn and grow together. Doing so will bolster your students' confidence, encourage more meaningful conversations, and bring the entire family along on their journey into Scripture.

 ### Closing Prayer

Close in prayer or have the students take turns leading the closing prayer each week. Some groups are comfortable praying together, while others may have some students who are more introverted or who are not yet comfortable praying aloud or being "put on the spot." Discern your group's comfort level and decide accordingly. If you decide to ask students to lead prayer, be sure to ask them ahead of time so they can prepare properly. Additionally, be sure to ask different personality types to lead, including both outgoing students as well as quieter ones.

---

Teaching guidelines for individual sessions can be found in
"Part Four: *Encounter* Student Workbook Sessions One to Eight."

---

# TIPS FOR LEADING A MIDDLE-SCHOOL BIBLE STUDY

Doing these things when leading your middle-school youth into Sacred Scripture will increase your effectiveness:

1. **Make them comfortable**

   This age group is going through constant change—emotionally, socially, and physically. They often are not comfortable in their own skin, much less in a classroom or "church hall" setting.

   Do everything you can to create an environment where they can relax and get comfortable. You can do this by offering refreshments and more comfortable chairs to sit on. Anything you can do to make the environment more inviting will go a long way in helping students to join in.

   On the other hand, beware of anything that will cause more problems (couches instead of chairs) or that will lower their attention span (soda and high-sugar foods versus water and healthier snack foods).

2. **Ask thought-provoking questions**

   Give the students a chance to talk in a controlled setting. Ask questions that elicit a thoughtful response or begin healthy dialogue. Avoid questions with a "yes" or "no" answer ("Have you ever …?" or "Do you like it when …?"), which invite digression and make the facilitator's job more challenging. Instead, ask questions like, "How did you feel when …?" or "What would you do if …?"

3. **Respect their challenges**

   Try to avoid examples that begin with, "When I was your age …" Youth today are surrounded by more technology, more easily accessible temptation, and more immorality than ever before. Likening your upbringing to theirs quickly antiquates you in the minds of most middle-school students. Showing respect for how challenging their faith walk can be is a great way to earn their respect for you as a leader. If you share stories from your own youth, it will help them to really engage in what you're saying if you acknowledge how much more challenging it is for them today.

4. **Till the soil**

   Don't rush through the opening prayer times. Be sure to ask them to share their own intentions before you begin to pray. Invite them to share a petition. Remind them that you pray for them. At each meeting, be sure to check back in on how the youth (and their families) are doing with the petitions they have shared previously. The more you till the soil of adolescent hearts, the greater attention they will pay during the session and the more deeply they will share during discussions. Listen to them if you want them to listen to you.

5. **Encourage but don't "push"**

   We all want our young people to get excited about their faith and to "get it." There is a fine line, however, between encouraging and pushing youth too hard. Don't let your desire for them to engage allow you to forget that, while you're dealing with one collective group of souls, each participant is on his or her own journey with God. Treat them as individuals. Have "goals" for each student you are leading. For some, who have been raised in the Faith or who are more outgoing, sharing not only comes easily but is second nature. For others, who are shy or for whom theology is more of a second or third "language," merely getting them to read aloud or share publicly is a huge victory. Discern where each youth is, and walk alongside your students at a pace that affirms as well as challenges them.

6. **Don't confuse "silence" with boredom**

   It's ironic how so many of us desire more silence for (and from) our youth, yet when they achieve such a feat in a classroom or youth-group setting, it often makes us nervous. It's possible that your students may be bored, or maybe they're just thinking. Try to discern what is happening by watching their body language and paying attention to what they do and do not say. Their silence might be a good sign, an indication that they are actively processing and ruminating on what has been shared. Oftentimes, when the Spirit is making that trip from their heads to their hearts, preteens are unable to properly articulate or process what God is doing—even adults struggle with this. Their body language will tell you if your message is "getting through" or if you're missing the mark.

7. **Offer authentic affirmation**

   Affirmation does more than win you favor; it ensures attentiveness and encourages participation. Affirm your young people every chance you get, but be sure it's authentic affirmation ... words of praise that go beyond conversational "niceties" or peripherals about their hair or their clothes. Praise them when they participate. Acknowledge their responses (even if they are incorrect) as a good example of thought processing. Affirm their courage in sharing something of depth and participating in prayer. Offer a kind word when they read well, when they engage in intelligent conversation, and when they are respectful of your opinions and the opinions of others. Affirmation goes a long way in opening the hearts and minds of adolescents.

# Part Four
## *ENCOUNTER* STUDENT WORKBOOK
## SESSIONS ONE TO EIGHT

On the following pages, each page of the *Encounter* Student Workbook is reproduced in miniature. Step-by-step instructions are provided alongside each page for you, the leader, along with pertinent teaching aids.

A general explanation of parts and features of the Student Workbook is on pages L-7 through L-10 of this Leader's Guide.

**To prepare for each class:** Read the instructions surrounding the appropriate pages taken from the Student Workbook and watch the video to learn how they fit together.

Are you ready? Turn the page, and let's go!

These pages are from the Student Workbook

**Main point of this Welcome:**
God—who knows them better than anyone on earth (including their parents)—wants to have a deeper relationship with them. Through Scripture, we get to know God—and ourselves—better.

# Welcome
(A LETTER FROM MARK HART)

There are a lot of ways you can get to know people, but nothing works like sitting with someone one-on-one and talking together. That person can't really know you, either, until you share from your heart.

There is one important exception, someone who knows all about you and loves you more than life itself. No, not Santa Claus, and not your parents. It's God, the author of your life. That's right, God is the author, and you are a character in his story. And if you really want to know yourself, the best and fastest way to do that is to get to know the one who created you.

The Bible is a great way to get to know God and the kind of Father he is. You'll also get to know a lot of his children. Everyone you encounter in the Bible is worth learning from in some way. You'll soon realize that living as a Christian is not so much about "finding yourself" as it is about finding and unleashing Christ's power within you. The more you recognize God's presence in your life, the better you'll be able to share his love with others.

The secret to a joyful life and a hope-filled future isn't about figuring out tomorrow; it's about listening to God today. God, the author of life, has something to say to you through the brothers and sisters who went before you. So take a deep breath and turn the page—it's story time!

God bless you!

*Mark Hart*
Mark Hart

# Session One

 **Welcome**

As class begins, have students look at their Student Workbooks and put their names on the front. Explain that these workbooks are going to be used in class—that they will write in their books as prompted by the speaker, Mark Hart.

**Next, read "Welcome: A Letter from Mark Hart."**
Depending on the maturity and comfort level of your group, you may choose a volunteer to read it aloud as the class follows along, or have them read it silently before engaging them in discussion with questions such as …

- "What questions do you ask when you want to get to know someone?"
- "As you get to know someone better, what else do you talk about?"

- "Can someone have 1,000 Facebook 'friends' who are really friends? Why or why not?"*
- "What's the difference between 'kind of' knowing someone and a real friend?"

**\* Note:** The idea is to have them explain in their own words the difference between relationships that are shallow in nature and relationships that go deeper. Middle-school girls will most likely be far more interactive and responsive to this approach than boys, but it will still get the boys thinking. This approach is particularly effective in a smaller classroom or a youth-group format where the kids really "know" one another and are more likely to share freely.

# Session One

• AN INTRODUCTION TO THE BIBLE

You'll open a lot of books in your lifetime—textbooks, yearbooks, comic books, maybe art and poetry books. You already know how much you *love* lugging around textbooks in your backpack for studying. But did a textbook ever change your life?

On the other hand, maybe you're an avid reader, and your room is full of books. Or maybe you prefer to read everything on a screen. Whatever the case, there is one book that is different from any other. It's the best-selling book in history, published in every language on the planet, and available in almost every corner of the earth (even in places where it is still illegal). That book is the Bible.

The Bible is different from any other book you'll ever read. It's not just words *about* God. Scripture is the Word *of* God, and that difference is huge.

Other books might help you learn about the Bible, like this study will. But nothing, no other book, no study, no pamphlet, will ever give you what the Bible can … for when you read the Bible yourself, something amazing happens.

God blesses you in a very special way, and his life (grace) fills you in a new way.

Forget what you've heard or learned about the Bible in the past. Forget how you felt in the past about reading Scripture on your own. As we begin, ask the Holy Spirit, the actual author of Scripture, to open your mind, your eyes, your ears, and your heart as we move forward, now. Your life is about to change for the better.

Let's have some fun …

From this point on, Leader's Guide page numbers and Student Workbook page numbers will match.

## Themes: Session One

- "She-bears and a dead man": The Bible is alive with exciting stories!
- The Bible is a light that helps us navigate the darkness.
- Read the Bible to "encounter" God in history and in our lives.

VERSE TO REMEMBER

" … you will know the truth, and the truth will make you free."

John 8:32

1

 **Opening Prayer**

Before you pray, spend about twenty seconds in silence, encouraging students to eliminate any distractions and to open their hearts to what God wants to share with them in this study.

*"Lord, thank you for all of our blessings. Thank you for each and every soul in this room and for our families. Thank you for all of the gifts you've given us, especially for all those gifts we sometimes take for granted. Help us never to forget how much you love us, Father. And as we begin this study, we say thank you for the gift of your Church, our Catholic Faith, and for your Holy Scriptures. We ask the Holy Spirit to open our eyes and minds and hearts, now, to help us encounter you in a new way. And we ask all these prayers in Jesus' name. Amen."*

 **Introduce the Session and the "Verse to Remember."**

- Have a volunteer read the introduction to Session One aloud or read it together silently.
- Have students read the "Verse to Remember" aloud together and write in the reference (John 8:32).
- Tell the kids to turn the page when you are ready to start the video.

When it's time for students to take the "Pop Quiz," Mark will prompt you to stop the DVD. (Mark does NOT go over the answers on the DVD because the point of the exercise is simply to demonstrate to the class how much more they know about pop culture than they do about the Catholic Faith—something to think about changing. The answers are provided for you below in case you want to review them with the class before you restart the DVD.)

Twelve time periods and fourteen "narrative books" make up the *Great Adventure Bible Timeline.*

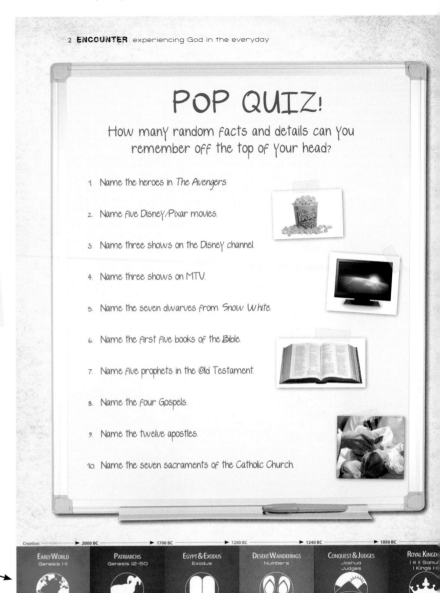

## Quiz Answers

1. Captain America, Iron Man, Thor, the Hulk, Black Widow, Hawkeye

2. • *Toy Story (1-3)*
   • *A Bug's Life*
   • *Monsters, Inc.*
   • *Finding Nemo*
   • *The Incredibles*
   • *Cars 1 & 2*
   • *Ratatouille*
   • *WALL-E*
   • *Up*
   • *Brave*
   • *Monsters University*

3. Check local listings – shows vary from year to year.

4. Check local listings – shows vary from year to year.

5. Bashful, Doc, Dopey, Grumpy, Happy, Sleepy & Sneezy

6. Genesis, Exodus, Leviticus, Numbers, Deuteronomy

7. Moses, Elijah, Elisha, Isaiah, Jeremiah, Ezekiel, Daniel, Hosea, Joel, Amos, Obadiah, Jonah, Micah, Nahum, Habakkuk, Zephaniah, Haggai, Zechariah, Malachi

8. Matthew, Mark, Luke & John

9. Simon Peter, Andrew, John, James, Phillip, Bartholomew (also called Nathanael), Matthew (also called Levi), Thomas, James (the lesser, the son of Alphaeus), Simon (the Zealot), Jude (also called Thaddeus, the son of James) and Judas Iscariot

10. Baptism, Holy Communion, confirmation, confession, anointing of the sick, holy matrimony, holy orders

**Step 4** **Show DVD "Session One: An Introduction to the Bible"**

Before you start the DVD, explain that "Breaking It Down" is a feature of every session. During the DVD, Mark will ask the questions and tell them what to write down, and the answers will pop up on the screen. Be ready to prompt the students as needed, if they miss it! Tips for you are in the left and right margins above.

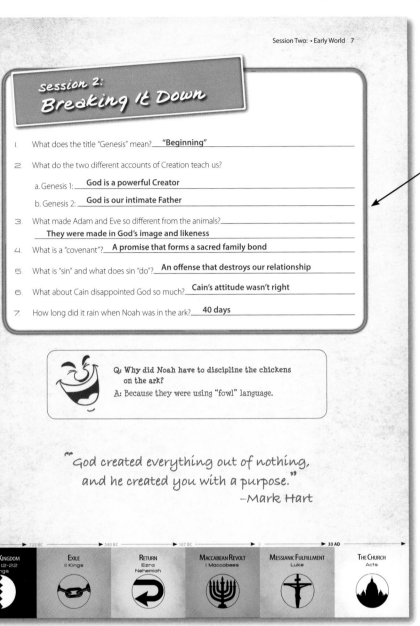

Session Two: • Early World 7

## session 2:
## Breaking It Down

1. What does the title "Genesis" mean? **"Beginning"**

2. What do the two different accounts of Creation teach us?

 a. Genesis 1: **God is a powerful Creator**

 b. Genesis 2: **God is our intimate Father**

3. What made Adam and Eve so different from the animals? **They were made in God's image and likeness**

4. What is a "covenant"? **A promise that forms a sacred family bond**

5. What is "sin" and what does sin "do"? **An offense that destroys our relationship**

6. What about Cain disappointed God so much? **Cain's attitude wasn't right**

7. How long did it rain when Noah was in the ark? **40 days**

Q: Why did Noah have to discipline the chickens on the ark?

A: Because they were using "fowl" language.

"God created everything out of nothing, and he created you with a purpose."
—Mark Hart

722 BC ———— 540 BC ———— 167 BC ———— 0 ———— 33 AD

| D KINGDOM s 12-22 Kings | EXILE II Kings | RETURN Ezra Nehemiah | MACCABEAN REVOLT I Maccabees | MESSIANIC FULFILLMENT Luke | THE CHURCH Acts |

Until students are used to filling out these answers each week, you may need to prompt them. Consider reviewing answers after the DVD if some have trouble getting them down.

Four ways humans image God: rational souls, intellect, free will, and capacity to love.

 **Talking It Out (After the DVD)**
Step 5

1. What would you have done if you were Adam or Eve and the serpent had spoken to you?

2. How do you struggle with being obedient? To God? To your parents? To your teachers and other leaders?

3. How would you describe "sin" in your own words to someone who didn't know what it was?

4. Are you more like Cain or Abel most days? Explain your answer.

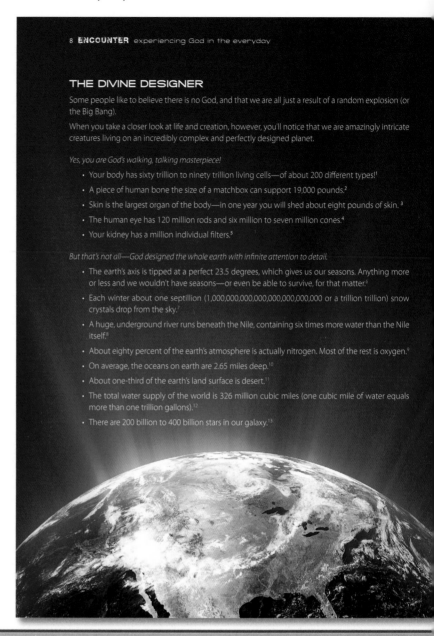

8 **ENCOUNTER** experiencing God in the everyday

## THE DIVINE DESIGNER

Some people like to believe there is no God, and that we are all just a result of a random explosion (or the Big Bang).

When you take a closer look at life and creation, however, you'll notice that we are amazingly intricate creatures living on an incredibly complex and perfectly designed planet.

*Yes, you are God's walking, talking masterpiece!*

- Your body has sixty trillion to ninety trillion living cells—of about 200 different types![1]
- A piece of human bone the size of a matchbox can support 19,000 pounds.[2]
- Skin is the largest organ of the body—in one year you will shed about eight pounds of skin. [3]
- The human eye has 120 million rods and six million to seven million cones.[4]
- Your kidney has a million individual filters.[5]

*But that's not all—God designed the whole earth with infinite attention to detail.*

- The earth's axis is tipped at a perfect 23.5 degrees, which gives us our seasons. Anything more or less and we wouldn't have seasons—or even be able to survive, for that matter.[6]
- Each winter about one septillion (1,000,000,000,000,000,000,000,000 or a trillion trillion) snow crystals drop from the sky.[7]
- A huge, underground river runs beneath the Nile, containing six times more water than the Nile itself.[8]
- About eighty percent of the earth's atmosphere is actually nitrogen. Most of the rest is oxygen.[9]
- On average, the oceans on earth are 2.65 miles deep.[10]
- About one-third of the earth's land surface is desert.[11]
- The total water supply of the world is 326 million cubic miles (one cubic mile of water equals more than one trillion gallons).[12]
- There are 200 billion to 400 billion stars in our galaxy.[13]

 **Taking It Home**

Step 6

Use this as a conversation starter. Using these scientific facts, draw the parallel between the world they see and the God "they don't." The more intentionally you can show God to be the Creator of all things, the more the students will begin to encounter God in everything from a sunset to a mountain to a newborn baby.

Ask the students where else they see the hand of God in the world around them. Encourage them to give specific examples of some of the most beautiful things they have seen that God has created. Affirm their own beauty, reminding them that God is perfect and does not make mistakes. Their lives echo God's love and greatness. This point is particularly important to make with students in this age group, who often stare into a mirror pointing out "everything God did wrong" (in their opinion), missing the image of God staring back at them.

Review the "Verse to Remember" (page 5). What do the students take from it, now that they have heard Mark's talk?

 **Closing Prayer**

Step 7

Choose a prayer that invokes the image of God as Creator, such as Psalm 136, or go around the circle and have each student thank God for some part of his creation.

# Session Three

- PATRIARCHS
- EGYPT & EXODUS (PART I)

**Books: Genesis 12–50, Exodus**

Nobody's family is perfect. Sure, you might look around at your friends' families and wish you had one like theirs (or thank God that you don't). The thing is, it's important to look at your own family in order to love and understand them as God calls you to do.

Do you spend more time upset about how things are or on working to love your family members better? Do you focus more on what you don't have in your family or on thanking God for all you *do* have?

As you'll hear in this session, families have been messed up for thousands of years. Sometimes it's their fault and sometimes it's not, but God is always reaching out and encouraging us to get better.

God isn't far away. These chapters remind us that God is very much present in our day-to-day lives; sometimes we just have to look harder to find him. Sometimes we have to be more patient, too.

When things don't go your way, do you trust God? Do you blame God? Do you doubt his love?

You're about to meet characters who did all three of these things. You can learn from all three types of responses. The choices you make will help determine the kind of life you are going to have: a life filled with joy or a life filled with sorrow.

The choice is yours. So, let's get to it!

---

**VERSE TO REMEMBER**

"The LORD will fight for you, and you have only to be still."

Exodus 14:14

---

9

---

**Themes: Session Three**

- God has a mission and purpose for you, just like he had plans for Abraham and Moses.
- Testings and trials strengthen us and lead to God's blessing.
- Even when you mess up, God loves you and will fight the battle for you.

---

# Session Three

 **Welcome**

- Reward anyone who can recite last week's "Verse to Remember" (Genesis 1:27) or answer the Question of the Week (chosen from the last session). This week's question might be something like "How many days did the rain fall to produce the great Flood, and how did Noah and his family escape?" (40 days, in an ark.)
- Introduce *Bible Timeline* periods and narrative books for Session Three. (Point them out in the Student Workbook.)

 **Opening Prayer**

*"Lord God, thank you for our families. Thank you for those family members who love us well and even those family members who are difficult to love. Lord, please help us to be a light within our homes and extended families. Help us to be more patient, more forgiving, and more compassionate. Help us to build up with our words and never to tear down. Help us to trust, Lord, even when we don't understand some of the things that happen in our homes and relationships. Mother Mary and St. Joseph, please pray with us, now, that we would help create families that resemble your own holy family. Hail Mary …"*

 **Introduction/ "Verse to Remember"**

- Have a volunteer read this introduction aloud or read it together silently.
- Have students read the verse aloud together and write in the reference.

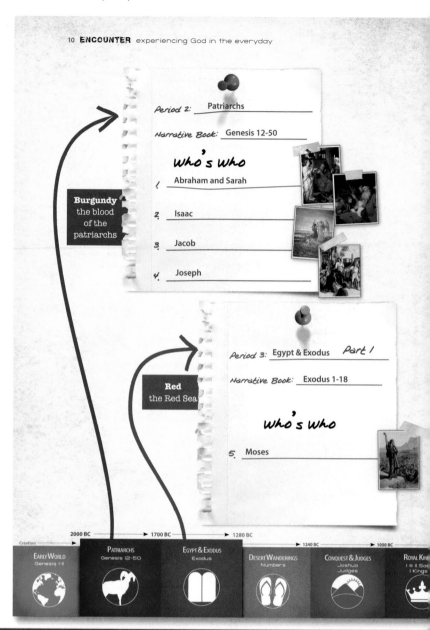

## Key Events: Patriarchs

- Covenant with Abraham (Genesis 15; 17:1-11)
- The sacrifice of Isaac (Genesis 22:1-19)
- Joseph's brothers sell him out (Genesis 37:12-36)

## Key Events: Egypt & Exodus Part I

- Slavery in Egypt (Exodus 1:1-22)
- The burning bush (Exodus 3)
- The ten plagues (Exodus 7:1–11:10)
- Crossing the Red Sea (Exodus 13:17–15:21)

**Step 4** **Show DVD "Session Three: Patriarchs, Egypt and Exodus (Part 1)"**

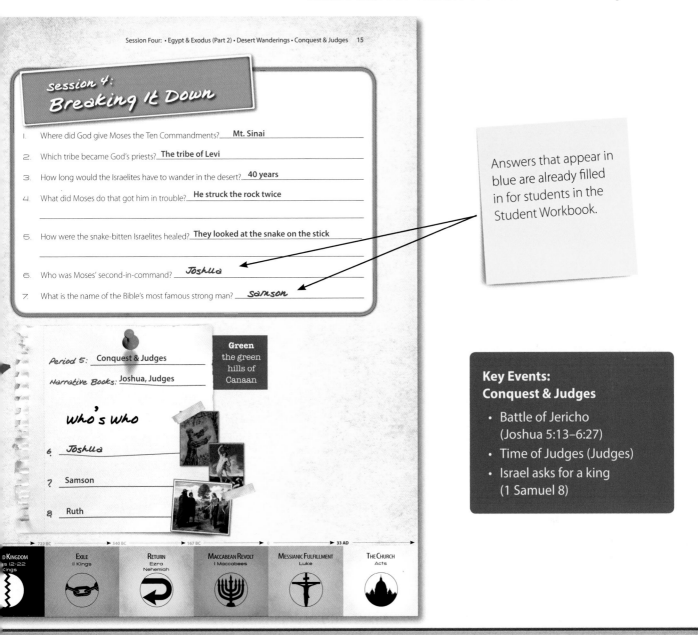

session 4:
**Breaking It Down**

1. Where did God give Moses the Ten Commandments?   Mt. Sinai

2. Which tribe became God's priests?   The tribe of Levi

3. How long would the Israelites have to wander in the desert?   40 years

4. What did Moses do that got him in trouble?   He struck the rock twice

5. How were the snake-bitten Israelites healed?   They looked at the snake on the stick

6. Who was Moses' second-in-command?   *Joshua*

7. What is the name of the Bible's most famous strong man?   *Samson*

Answers that appear in blue are already filled in for students in the Student Workbook.

Period 5:   Conquest & Judges

Narrative Books:   Joshua, Judges

**Green**
the green hills of Canaan

**Who's Who**

6.   *Joshua*

7.   Samson

8.   Ruth

**Key Events:**
**Conquest & Judges**

- Battle of Jericho
  (Joshua 5:13–6:27)
- Time of Judges (Judges)
- Israel asks for a king
  (1 Samuel 8)

| 722 BC | 540 BC | 167 BC | 0 | 33 AD |
|---|---|---|---|---|
| D KINGDOM gs 12-22 Kings | EXILE II Kings | RETURN Ezra Nehemiah | MACCABEAN REVOLT I Maccabees | MESSIANIC FULFILLMENT Luke | THE CHURCH Acts |

 **Step 5   Talking It Out (After the DVD)**

1. How would the world be different if everyone actually obeyed the Ten Commandments? Give examples.
2. Why was the Israelites' punishment of wandering in the desert so important for them? What was God trying to achieve through it?
3. What does Moses' punishment teach us about our relationship with God?
4. What can we learn about relationships from Samson and Delilah even today?

After the "man on the street" segment, you will be directed to pause the DVD. Have students turn to page 16 in their workbooks and write down as many of the commandments as they can before restarting the DVD. Answers and an "Examination of Conscience" are on pages 36-37.

**Consider sending home a note to parents this week,** explaining that the students learned about the Ten Commandments and the importance of the sacrament of reconciliation. Encourage them to make arrangements to go to confession as a family this week. Explain how important it is that parents create those opportunities without the kids having to ask.

16 **ENCOUNTER** experiencing God in the everyday

## LIST THE TEN COMMANDMENTS

When God gave Moses the Ten Commandments atop Mt. Sinai, he was doing more than giving all of us a list of "rules" to follow.

God wants us to be with him for eternity in heaven. The commandments are God's way of helping us live holier, more selfless lives—the commandments help us to become saints.

You probably know most (if not all) of the commandments. Do you know them in order?

List as many of the Ten Commandments as you can below, from memory.

**The Ten Commandments (Exodus 20):**

1. _____
2. _____
3. _____
4. _____
5. _____
6. _____
7. _____
8. _____
9. _____
10. _____

**How'd you do?**
Turn to page 36 to find out.

## Step 6  Taking It Home

This is a great time to talk to them about the importance of knowing and living the commandments. Encourage them to commit the Ten Commandments to memory, and let them know you will be quizzing them next week.

Talk with your students about the "Examination of Conscience" (page 37), and encourage them to take some time to examine their consciences thoroughly over the next few days. Have them ask the Lord where they need to change and to improve. Reaffirm to the students how vital the sacrament of penance is to their ongoing prayer life, and explain how God blesses each of them with grace to be stronger following the experience of reconciliation. Remind them that it's not enough to "know" the commandments with their heads; they also need to follow them with their hearts.

Review the "Verse to Remember" (page 13). What do the students take from it, now that they have heard Mark's talk?

## Step 7  Closing Prayer

This week, close by reviewing the Act of Contrition – consider having students copy it down in their workbooks as a learning exercise, if they do not already know it by heart:

*"Oh my God, I am sorry for my sins with all my heart. In choosing to do wrong and failing to do good, I have sinned against you whom I should love above all things. I firmly intend, with your help, to do penance, to sin no more, and to avoid whatever leads me to sin. Our Savior Jesus Christ suffered and died for us. In his name, my God, have mercy. Amen."*

# Session Five

- ROYAL KINGDOM
- DIVIDED KINGDOM

**Books: 1&2 Samuel, 1&2 Kings**

Have you ever said to yourself, "*If I could just* (insert desired thing here) … *then I'd be happy.*"

Some people insert "be popular" or "become famous." Some people say "be smarter" or "be more athletic." I used to say "grow taller" and "get better-looking." My acne was so bad at one point I didn't even want to go to school. I was so stressed about how I compared to others, that it affected everything about me—what I wore, what music I listened to, and even what sports and activities I took part in.

I was more worried about how others saw me than I was about what God thought of me.

I wish I'd read these chapters we're about to walk through when I was in middle school. They remind us about what matters most. They echo what we learned in those first couple of sessions of the Timeline, about where our worth comes from and, more to the point, *who* it comes from.

This session will remind you, too, that you are capable of way more than you might think … as long as you keep God first in your life.

No mountain is too tall, no fear too big, no opponent too scary, if God is in your corner.

We're also going to see what happens when we put God second, third, or last. We'll see how badly things go when we rely too much on our own talents and skills and not on the one who gave them to us.

Buckle up, brothers and sisters—this session has more drama than any reality show.

*VERSE TO REMEMBER*

"*Before I formed you in the womb I knew you, and before you were born I consecrated you …*"

*Jeremiah 1:5*

17

## Themes: Session Five

- When we sin, God gives us a chance to start over.
- Every life is a precious gift from God. He has a plan for each of us.
- The prophets (prophet means "mouthpiece") courageously carried God's message, though it sometimes put them in a difficult place. We need to speak the truth with courage, too.

---

# Session Five

 **Welcome**
Step 1

- Reward anyone who can recite last week's "Verse to Remember" (1 Samuel 16:7). For the Question of the Week, it's "quiz time"! See how many of the Ten Commandments your students can recall—in order, from memory.
- Introduce *Bible Timeline* periods and narrative books for Session Five.

Step 2 **Opening Prayer**

*"Holy Spirit, help us to become more holy. Show us who we were created to be and what we are created to do in this world. Reveal our gifts and our talents to us, not so we can focus on ourselves, but so we can use those gifts and talents to lead others to you. Help us to find ourselves in each of the stories we will study today. Thank you for our Holy Father, bishops, priests, deacons, religious, and all who lead us closer to you. Be with us during this time of study, Lord, so that we can begin to listen even more closely to what your plans are for our lives. And may this time in your Word help us to grow stronger in our faith. Glory be …"*

 **Introduction/"Verse to Remember"**
Step 3

- Have a volunteer read the introduction aloud or read it together silently.
- Have students read the verse aloud together and write in the reference.

**Key Events: Royal Kingdom**
- David kills Goliath (1 Samuel 17)
- Covenant with David (2 Samuel 7)
- First Temple built (1 Kings 5–8)

When God tells David he will "build David a house" that will last forever (2 Samuel 7:11b-16), he is referring to the Davidic dynasty and ultimately to Christ ruling on the throne.

At the beginning of the session, prompt students to write the names of the narrative books in the correct spaces: "Royal Kingdom" is 1 & 2 Samuel and 1 Kings 1–11; "Divided Kingdom" is 1 Kings 12–22 and 2 Kings. (Mark goes through this quickly.)

18 **ENCOUNTER** experiencing God in the everyday

session 5:
*Breaking It Down*

1. What was the name of Israel's first king? _saul_
2. What was David's first teenage job? **Shepherd**
3. What army did Goliath fight for? **The Philistines**
4. What friend did David betray? **Uriah**
5. Which king built God's Temple? **Solomon**
6. When did the kingdom divide into two? **930 BC**
7. What does the word "prophet" mean? **"Mouthpiece"**

*Period 6:* Royal Kingdom
*Narrative Books:* 1 & 2 Samuel
1 Kings 1-11

who's who

**Purple** royalty

1. Saul
2. David
3. solomon

1250 BC

Creation   2000 BC   1700 BC   1280 BC   1240 BC

EARLY WORLD
Genesis 1-11

PATRIARCHS
Genesis 12-50

EGYPT & EXODUS
Exodus

DESERT WANDERINGS
Numbers

CONQUEST & JUDGES
Joshua
Judges

ROYAL KINGDOM
1 & II Samuel
1 Kings 1-11

 **Step 4** **Show DVD "Session Five: Royal Kingdom"**

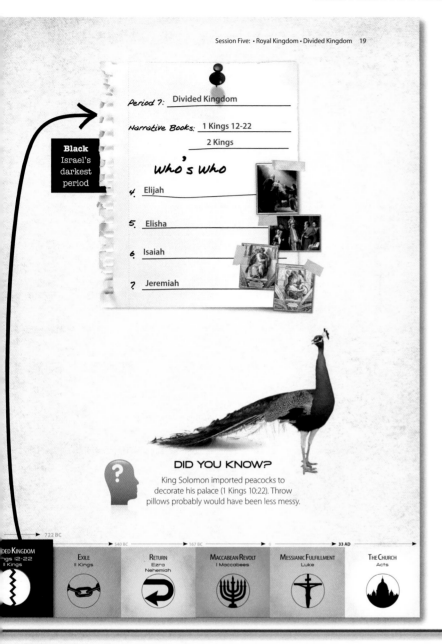

*Period 7:* Divided Kingdom

*Narrative Books:* 1 Kings 12-22
2 Kings

### who's who

4. Elijah

5. Elisha

6. Isaiah

7. Jeremiah

**Black**
Israel's darkest period

**DID YOU KNOW?**
King Solomon imported peacocks to decorate his palace (1 Kings 10:22). Throw pillows probably would have been less messy.

**Key Events: Divided Kingdom**
- The kingdom divides (1 Kings 12:16-20)
- A fish catches Jonah (Jonah)
- Jeremiah follows God (Jeremiah)

Turn the page for a map of the Divided Kingdom.

722 BC                540 BC        167 BC        0        33 AD

| DIVIDED KINGDOM Kings 12-22 II Kings | EXILE II Kings | RETURN Ezra Nehemiah | MACCABEAN REVOLT I Maccabees | MESSIANIC FULFILLMENT Luke | THE CHURCH Acts |

## Step 5 — Talking It Out (After the DVD)

1. Discuss the battle between David and Goliath. Ask your students if they have ever been "dismissed" by an adult because they are (or appear to be) too young? Let them share what happened to them and how it made them feel.

2. Ask them for some examples—in their own lives—of "giants" they were fearful of, but overcame.

3. David was a great military leader but struggled personally and in his relationships. Ask what qualities are essential for a good leader. Ask them for examples of strong leadership that they have seen in their own lives.

4. Being a prophet of God was not easy. People usually don't like to hear the truth of God. Ask the students who they have seen or heard share truth often and who, if any, received a hard time because of it?

5. Ask them, "Would you want to be a prophet? Why or why not?"

**The Divided Kingdom**

- Northern Kingdom: Israel (ten tribes); capital: Samaria
- Southern Kingdom: Judah (two tribes); capital: Jerusalem
- Note that the Temple (in Jerusalem) is in the South. The Northern Kingdom set up centers of worship at Dan and Bethel. This will cause them big problems!

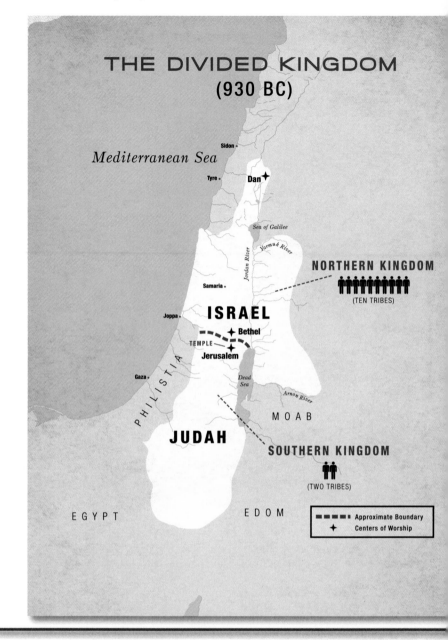

## Step 6 — Taking It Home

Point out the main features of this map to give the students a visual of the Divided Kingdom (see above).

Now that you are several sessions into *Encounter*, consider adding one or more of these activities:

- Have them learn the prophetic books (Isaiah through Malachi) in order, using their Bible's table of contents. Offer a prize the following week for those who achieve it.
- Have a large-group "rap session" about what they have learned about Scripture and, more importantly, about themselves in the past few weeks.
- Ask what specific intentions they need prayers for, and spend time as a group in prayer.

- Take a look at the upcoming Sunday Gospel reading and reflect on it as a group, tying in the Bible verses you're studying with the Bible verses they will hear at Mass.
- Have some fun and ask some "quiz-type" questions based on the first five sessions. Reward them for what they have retained.
- Do something to acknowledge how much your students have learned to keep them excited for the final three weeks.

Review the "Verse to Remember" (page 17). What do the students take from it, now that they have heard Mark's talk?

## Step 7 — Closing Prayer

King David was not just a warrior—he was also a great musician and poet, who wrote many of the psalms. This week, choose one of your favorite psalms to share with the students as the closing prayer.

# Session Six

- EXILE
- RETURN
- MACCABEAN REVOLT

**Books:** 2 Kings, Ezra, Nehemiah, 1 Maccabees

You'll have a lot of different types of friends in your lifetime. Some you'll have for life, others for a shorter time. You'll have friendships that fade as soon as bad times happen, and friendships that withstand just about anything. The key is to find people who build you up, not tear you down.

This session is going to reveal a lot about what it means to be faithful—to God, to family, and to friends.

The best gift you can ever give someone else is to lead that person's soul closer to God. It's the only gift that keeps giving, for eternity. Stop and think about your life for a moment. Do most of your friends lead you closer to God or further away from his love?

Now ask yourself what kind of friend you are. Do you lead your friends—through your words and your actions—closer to God or further away from him?

These aren't stupid questions, and they aren't for immature souls. These realities matter in life. What kind of friends you choose to hang out with and the kind of friend you choose to be makes all the difference in this world … and in the next.

We're about to see what it means to be a *faithful* friend. The book of Sirach says that when you find a faithful friend, "you find a treasure" (Sirach 6:14, NAB). These chapters will affirm that truth and challenge your own friendships, if you let them.

Let's see how we measure up to those who went before us and did it right.

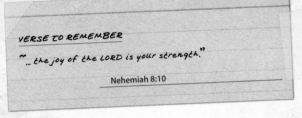

VERSE TO REMEMBER

"… the joy of the LORD is your strength."

Nehemiah 8:10

21

## Themes: Session Six

- The word *canon* means "measuring rod." All 73 books in the Catholic Bible—including the seven deutero-canonical books—"measured up."
- Everything in the Temple reminded the Israelites of their covenant with God; everything in our church reminds us of Christ and of the family of God.
- Importance of the Sabbath and of spending time with family as foundational to a happy life.
- The stories of Queen Esther and the Maccabees remind us of the importance of having moral courage—of standing for what is right (something we can accomplish through the grace of God).

---

# Session Six:

 **Welcome**

- Reward anyone who can recite last week's "Verse to Remember" (Jeremiah 1:5) or answer the Question of the Week chosen from last week's lesson. (For example, "Where did Jonah refuse to go, that prompted God to have him swallowed by the great fish?" Nineveh.)
- Introduce *Bible Timeline* periods and narrative books for this Session Six.

 **Opening Prayer**

*"Lord, when life gets hard, help me to trust you more. Help me to run to you when I'm struggling. Remind me of your love, Jesus, when I just can't feel it. When temptations come my way, Holy Spirit, help me to be strong. When I feel lost and alone, Mother Mary, please pray with me and help me to more clearly see your Son Jesus' face and to hear his voice. As I grow older, help me be like a child in my faith, always running to my Father and trusting in his love for me. Our Father …"*

 **Introduction/ "Verse to Remember"**

- Have a volunteer read this introduction aloud or read it together silently.
- Have students read the verse aloud together and write in the reference.

"Shack, Rack, and Ben" = Shadrach, Meshach, and Abednego.

### Key Events: Exile

- Israel falls to Assyria (2 Kings 17)
- Babylonian captivity (2 Kings 25)
- The fiery furnace (Daniel 3)
- Daniel in the lion's den (Daniel 6)

### Key Events: Return

- The Jews return (Ezra 1)
- Zerubbabel rebuilds the Temple (Ezra 3–6)
- Nehemiah rebuilds the city walls (Nehemiah 3–4)
- Ezra reinstates the Law (Ezra 7–8)

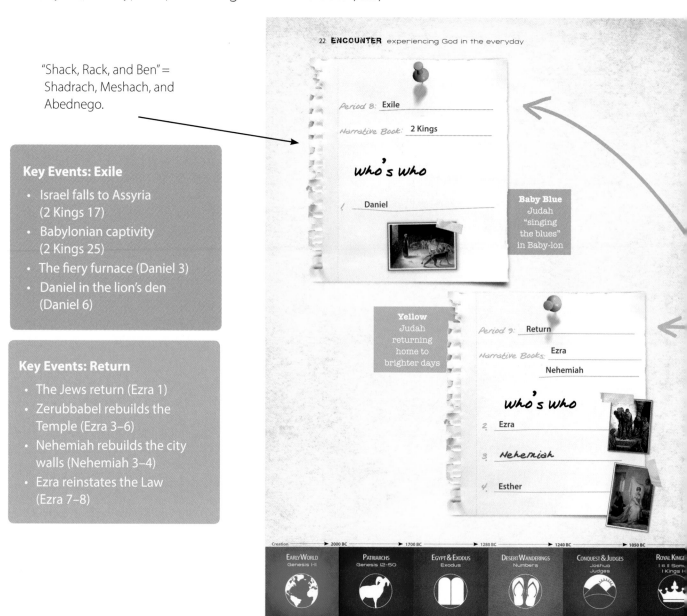

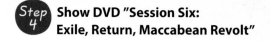

**Step 4** **Show DVD "Session Six: Exile, Return, Maccabean Revolt"**

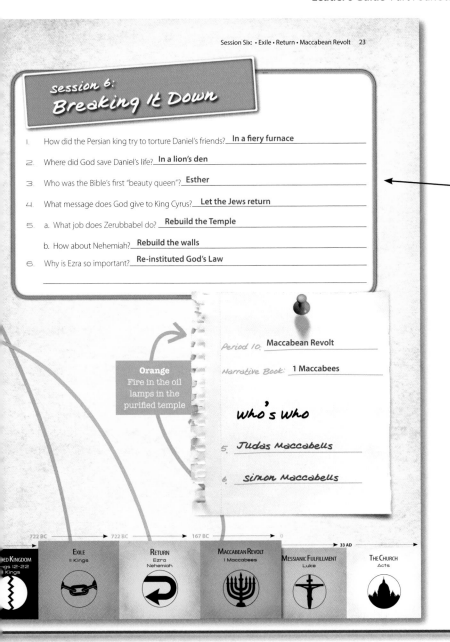

**session 6:**
**Breaking It Down**

1. How did the Persian king try to torture Daniel's friends? **In a fiery furnace**

2. Where did God save Daniel's life? **In a lion's den**

3. Who was the Bible's first "beauty queen"? **Esther**

4. What message does God give to King Cyrus? **Let the Jews return**

5. a. What job does Zerubbabel do? **Rebuild the Temple**

   b. How about Nehemiah? **Rebuild the walls**

6. Why is Ezra so important? **Re-instituted God's Law**

The world's first beauty queen, Queen Esther, is introduced late in the video "out of order" by Mark, as an icon (like the Maccabees) of standing up for truth.

**Orange**
Fire in the oil lamps in the purified temple

*Period 10:* **Maccabean Revolt**

*Narrative Book:* **1 Maccabees**

*Who's Who*

5. *Judas Maccabeus*

6. *Simon Maccabeus*

**Key Events: Maccabean Revolt**
- Greece demands pagan worship (1 Maccabees 1)
- The Maccabees fight back (1 Maccabees 2–4)
- Rededication of the Temple (Hanukkah) (1 Maccabees 4:36-61)

722 BC   722 BC   167 BC   0   33 AD

| ...ED KINGDOM ...gs 12-22 ...I Kings | EXILE II Kings | RETURN Ezra Nehemiah | MACCABEAN REVOLT I Maccabees | MESSIANIC FULFILLMENT Luke | THE CHURCH Acts |

**Step 5   Talking It Out (After DVD)**

1. What do you think was going through Daniel's mind when he was thrown into the lion's den? What would you be thinking?

2. Esther and her people faced many challenges. What would you do if the government told you that you couldn't worship your God? Would it matter to you? How would you respond?

3. Why was it so important for Ezra to reintroduce the Law and Word of God when the people returned from exile?

4. The Maccabees stood up against a larger, stronger army. Give some situations in modern culture where we can show the same kind of courage the Maccabees showed.

24 **ENCOUNTER** experiencing God in the everyday

## MAJOR BIBLICAL EVENTS: OLD TESTAMENT REVIEW

### An *Encounter* Cheat Sheet

Everything that happens in the Bible is important, but there are some events in the Old Testament that you might want to be able to find quickly so you can study or read them on your own.

**Creation, Adam and Eve** (Genesis 1–3)

**Noah's Ark** (Genesis 6–9)

**Tower of Babel** (Genesis 11:1-9)

**The Destruction of Sodom and Gomorrah** (Genesis 19)

**Abraham Sacrifices Isaac** (Genesis 22:1-19)

**Jacob's Ladder** (Genesis 28)

**The Twelve Sons of Jacob, Joseph's Rise to Power** (Genesis 35–47)

**The Burning Bush** (Exodus 3)

**The Ten Plagues** (Exodus 7–12)

**The Crossing of the Red Sea** (Exodus 15)

**The Ten Commandments** (Exodus 20)

**The Battle of Jericho** (Joshua 6)

**The Story of Ruth and Boaz** (The Book of Ruth)

**Samson the Judge** (Judges 13–16)

**David and Goliath** (1 Samuel 17)

**Jonah and the Whale** (Jonah 1–2)

**Elijah on Mount Carmel** (1 Kings 18)

**Esther and the King** (The Book of Esther)

**Daniel and the Lion's Den** (Daniel 6)

**Maccabean Revolt** (1 Maccabees 1–4)

---

 **Taking It Home**

"Major Biblical Events: Old Testament Review" is a tool you can use to challenge your youth. There is so much to cover in these sessions, and the content is covered at such a rapid rate, that we don't get to read entire stories at length. With this list, all excuses evaporate.

Perhaps you pick one of the stories, ask how many details they remember from a previous session, and then read it aloud as a group. Maybe you challenge them to try to memorize the book and chapter for each major event—or as many of them as they can from the list. However you choose to use it, be sure to point them to this list and remind them that you're giving them the foundation, but that they are called to build on that foundation for the rest of their lives.

Review the "Verse to Remember" (page 21). What do the students take from it, now that they have heard Mark's talk?

 **Closing Prayer**

This week, you might choose a prayer by one of the "warrior saints" like this one:

> *"Teach us, good Lord,*
> *to serve you as you deserve,*
> *to give and not to count the cost,*
> *to fight and not to heed the wounds,*
> *to toil and not to seek for rest,*
> *to labor and not to ask for any reward*
> *save that of knowing that we do your will;*
> *through Jesus Christ our Lord, Amen."*
> *– St. Ignatius of Loyola*[1]

---

[1] *The Catholic Prayer Book,* Msgr. Michael Buckley, ed. (Ann Arbor, MI: Servant, 1986), 148.

# Session Seven

• MESSIANIC FULFILLMENT

**Book:** Luke

What do you believe about Jesus? What difference does it make in your life? These are the two most important decisions you will ever make.

That is absolutely true and important, so I'll say it again:

*What you believe about Jesus, and what difference that makes in your life, are the two most important decisions you will ever make.*

No other major religious leader (aside from some minor, crazy people) ever claimed to be God like Jesus Christ did. Some have claimed to have special insights into God, or to have spoken to God, or to be sent by God, but none of them actually claimed *to be God.*

Only the carpenter from Nazareth did that … and he died for it.

He rose because of it, too, and that fact changes everything.

Some people will say Jesus was a nice guy or a good teacher, but they won't admit he was God. The Gospels make it clear, though, that Jesus was the Christ, the Son of God. Just as he said he was.

We'll talk more about why we know that's true in this session.

The next question, though, is just as important: What difference does it make in your life?

Some people think it doesn't matter. Others refuse to "decide." Everyone is going to be held accountable, though, for what they have learned and how they have lived. And anyone living in the modern era, with access to the Internet, television, radio, and books has lost the excuse of ignorance.

What you believe about Jesus and how you live because of it have *eternal consequences* (as in, for all of eternity). This is huge.

If you were just a child, we wouldn't even be asking the question. You're not a child, though; you are a young man or a young woman. You are old enough to make an informed decision. It's time to grow up, spiritually, and ask some tough questions. It's also time to make some difficult decisions. No turning back.

The Lord is waiting for you with open arms. Let's take a step forward, today.

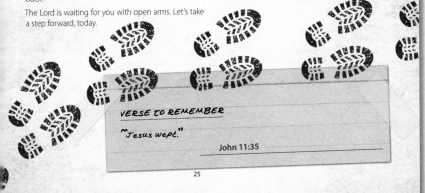

VERSE TO REMEMBER

"Jesus wept."

John 11:35

25

## Themes: Session Seven

• Jesus was tempted—and the devil will tempt you, too. That's why prayer is important.

• God has a message and a special task for you. Will you say "yes" to God?

• Through Jesus' sacrifice, we are restored to new life.

• Your role in the Church—how will you respond once you have encountered God in his Word?

Consider bringing a rosary for each student in your group. (See "Taking It Home," page 28.)

---

# Session Seven

 **Step 1 Welcome**

• Reward anyone who can recite last week's "Verse to Remember" (Nehemiah 8:10) or answer the Question of the Week (of your choice). For example, "What were the names of Daniel's three friends, and from what form of execution were they miraculously delivered? (Shadrach, Meshach, and Abednego were thrown into a fiery furnace.)

• Introduce the *Bible Timeline* period and narrative book for this session. "Messianic Fulfillment" covers the life and mission of Jesus Christ the Messiah.

 **Step 2 Opening Prayer**

*"Dear Jesus, I love you. Help me to want to know you better. Thank you for dying for my sins. Thank you for inviting me to live with you in heaven. Thank you for giving me your Mother to pray for me. Thank you for the gift of your Church and your Scriptures and the sacraments. Holy Spirit, please open my eyes to see Jesus in a new way during this study. Help me to follow Christ with my whole heart and to surrender my life to him. We ask all these things in Jesus' name. Amen."*

 **Step 3 Introduction/ "Verse to Remember"**

• Have a volunteer read this introduction aloud or read it together silently.

• Have students read the verse aloud together and write in the reference.

Mary is the Ark of the New Covenant, carrying within her Jesus, the Bread of Life and the Word of God, the great High Priest (as the Old Testament Ark carried manna, the Ten Commandments, and Aaron's budded rod).

The story of the disciples on the road to Emmaus is told in Luke 24:30-31.

26 **ENCOUNTER** experiencing God in the everyday

## session 7: Breaking It Down

1. Which of the Gospel writers were members of the original twelve apostles?_____
   Matthew and John

2. Why did God send an angel to Mary? (Why not a prophet?)_____
   God's news affects heaven and earth

3. What does the word "disciple" mean? **"Student"**

4. Why does Jesus choose twelve apostles? **There were 12 tribes of Israel**

5. What does "parable" mean? **"Comparison"**

6. Why did Jesus have to die? **To pay for our sins**

7. When do the Emmaus travelers recognize Jesus? **In the breaking of the bread**

*BRAIN TEASER*
*Name three consecutive days without using the words Wednesday, Friday, or Sunday.*

The Triduum.

| Creation | 2000 BC | 1700 BC | 1280 BC | 1240 BC | 1050 BC |
| EARLY WORLD Genesis 1-11 | PATRIARCHS Genesis 12-50 | EGYPT & EXODUS Exodus | DESERT WANDERINGS Numbers | CONQUEST & JUDGES Joshua Judges | ROYAL KIN I & II Sa I Kings |

 **Step 4** **Show DVD "Session Seven: Messianic Fulfillment"**

Now, open your Bible, pick a Gospel story, and work through the four steps:

**1. Read**

Select a passage and read it slowly. Get the basic "gist" of the story. Figure out the "who, what, when, where, why, and how" of it. After you've worked through it at least three or four times, you can move on to the next step.

**2. Reflect**

Now, what is the main "point" of what you read? What words jumped out at you? Which words "spoke" to your heart? Was it comforting, or did the passage make you uncomfortable, and why? If nothing jumps out at you, read it again, and ask how the passage applies to you, today, living in the twenty-first century. If you don't think it applies to you, look harder. This is where you really chew on the Gospel and ask yourself some questions.

**3. Respond**

Step three is where you and God speak together. If you're doing *lectio divina* alone, this is where you can *ask God questions* in your prayer. Anything that stood out to you in step two, bring to him now. Remember, it's important to listen in prayer, not just speak. Spend some time in silence and let God speak to your heart. Remember, this is about responding to God not only with your words, but with your heart. If you're doing *lectio divina* with a group, this is where you can discuss what the passage meant to you personally, what you liked, and what challenged you. Either way, it's important to listen to God speaking—to your heart or through other people.

**4. Rest**

During this final step, you just "rest." Now, that might be difficult for you. Don't let yourself get distracted. Be sure you're removed from screens and noise. This is where you really become a child again. It's like you're crawling up onto your heavenly Father's lap and letting him hold you. It might take some "practice" at first, just to sit with God and let him love you. Picture God staring into your eyes. Imagine him telling you how proud he is of you. Let him remind you how much you mean to him and all he desires for you. The first three steps help you to slow down as you realize different things (dots); this fourth step is where God will connect those dots, if you let him.

**CONTINUING THE JOURNEY**

Use these steps to meditate on the "Great Verses for Young Men and Women" on pages 40-41.

In class, use *lectio divina* to guide your students through this same passage. Pay attention to their responses and affirm their insights. Encourage them to try it on their own with a different story—perhaps the upcoming Sunday Gospel reading or a favorite from a past session. Create ways for the students to continue doing so in the weeks following the study (such as by meeting as a group or sharing through emails or social media avenues).

34 **ENCOUNTER** experiencing God in the everyday

Not ready to end the study just yet? Consider holding a follow-up session, and invite a man and woman (or two young adults) to present testimonies to your group on how Scripture challenges them and keeps them close to God. (Ask the man to address the boys, and the woman to address the girls.) Speaking about these types of verses with conviction creates a contagious atmosphere for both genders to grow in virtue. Do this in conjunction with the "Great Verses for Young Men and Young Women" on pages 40-41.

### MAJOR BIBLICAL EVENTS: NEW TESTAMENT REVIEW

**An *Encounter* Cheat Sheet**

The events listed below are not necessarily "more important" than others, but this list might help you track down some of the more famous scenes in the New Testament a little more quickly.

**Annunciation of Mary (and the angel speaks to Joseph):**
Luke 1:26-38
Matthew 1:18-25

**Birth of Christ:**
Luke 2:1-7

**Presentation in the Temple:**
Luke 2:22-29

**Baptism in the River Jordan:**
Matthew 3:13-17
Mark 1:9-11
Luke 3:21-22

**Fasting and Temptation in the wilderness:**
Matthew 4:1-11
Mark 1:12-13
Luke 4:1-13

**Wedding at Cana:**
John 2:1-12

**Sermon on the Mount:**
Matthew 5:1-12
Luke 6:17-49

**Peter is given the keys:**
Matthew 16:13-20

**Transfiguration:**
Matthew 17:1-9
Mark 9:2-9
Luke 9:28-36

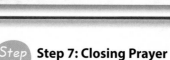

This list of major biblical events from the New Testament, like its Old Testament counterpart (following Session Six), is a handy, quick reference guide for any Catholic who wants to begin studying Scripture more intentionally. Encourage your youth to apply the lessons learned in their *lectio divina* training to stories from this list. It will offer them valuable direction and opportunities for prayer in the coming months when you as a leader will not be there to walk them through each one.

Review the "Verse to Remember" (page 29). What do the students take from it, now that they have heard Mark's talk?

**Step 7** **Step 7: Closing Prayer**

This week, encourage your students to recall some of what they learned from this study and to thank God for his love and care. Ask the Holy Spirit to come upon them and give them the courage and wisdom to follow Jesus every day and to love God and his Church.

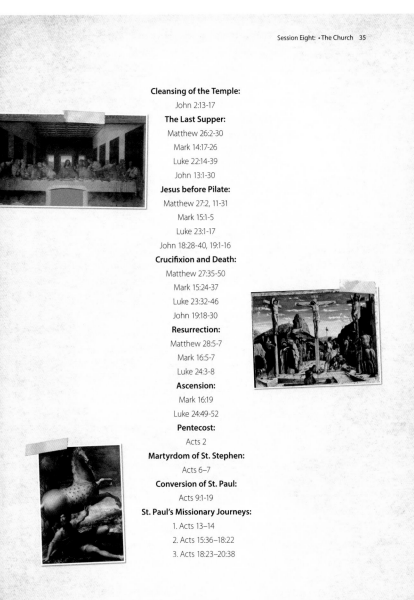

**Cleansing of the Temple:**
John 2:13-17

**The Last Supper:**
Matthew 26:2-30
Mark 14:17-26
Luke 22:14-39
John 13:1-30

**Jesus before Pilate:**
Matthew 27:2, 11-31
Mark 15:1-5
Luke 23:1-17
John 18:28-40, 19:1-16

**Crucifixion and Death:**
Matthew 27:35-50
Mark 15:24-37
Luke 23:32-46
John 19:18-30

**Resurrection:**
Matthew 28:5-7
Mark 16:5-7
Luke 24:3-8

**Ascension:**
Mark 16:19
Luke 24:49-52

**Pentecost:**
Acts 2

**Martyrdom of St. Stephen:**
Acts 6–7

**Conversion of St. Paul:**
Acts 9:1-19

**St. Paul's Missionary Journeys:**
1. Acts 13–14
2. Acts 15:36–18:22
3. Acts 18:23–20:38

Be sure to point out the other resources in "Continuing Your Journey," starting on page 40.

**Notes**

For use with Ten Commandments Quiz and activity at end of Session Four (page 16).

These two pages are available as a free download from BibleStudyforCatholics.com.

# Additional Session Resources

## THE TEN COMMANDMENTS

1. I AM THE LORD YOUR GOD. YOU SHALL WORSHIP THE LORD YOUR GOD AND HIM ONLY SHALL YOU SERVE.

2. YOU SHALL NOT TAKE THE NAME OF THE LORD YOUR GOD IN VAIN.

3. REMEMBER TO KEEP HOLY THE SABBATH DAY.

4. HONOR YOUR FATHER AND YOUR MOTHER.

5. YOU SHALL NOT KILL.

6. YOU SHALL NOT COMMIT ADULTERY.

7. YOU SHALL NOT STEAL.

8. YOU SHALL NOT BEAR FALSE WITNESS AGAINST YOUR NEIGHBOR.

9. YOU SHALL NOT COVET YOUR NEIGHBOR'S WIFE.

10. YOU SHALL NOT COVET YOUR NEIGHBOR'S GOODS.

It's important to realize that living by these commandments is more the "minimum" expectation of a Christian's ordinary, everyday behavior. Jesus reminds us of the importance of the Ten Commandments when he speaks to the rich young man (Matthew 19:16-22), but he also notes that the young man must surrender *everything* and follow him if he wants to experience eternal life.

Each of these commandments actually "covers" a variety of sins and warnings. Take some time to read through Part Three of the *Catechism of the Catholic Church*.

You might also notice that some Christians number the Ten Commandments differently than we Catholics do. The Catholic Tradition uses the division listed above, given to us by St. Augustine. Some Christian denominations number them differently. It's important to note, however, that this list is the one established by the early Church and handed on to us today.

If you can commit these to memory and live them out daily, you're well on your way to sainthood. Maybe you'll even get your own statue someday. (How cool would that be?)

**Notes**

# EXAMINATION OF CONSCIENCE

In order to make a good confession, it's important to take time to do an examination of conscience. An examination is designed to help you recall anything and everything you've done that violated God's commandments, times when you failed to love God and others with your whole mind, heart, and strength.

Take some time to pray through the following questions, and give the Holy Spirit permission to reveal to your heart all those ways that you've fallen short of how God is calling you to live.

Spend some time repenting for your sins in your heart and preparing yourself to confess your sins during the sacrament of confession.

### First and Second Commandments

"I am the LORD your God. You shall worship the Lord your God and him only shall you serve." "You shall not take the name of the Lord your God in vain." Do you blaspheme the name of God with your words and insults? Do you curse or use foul language against God or neighbor?

### Third Commandment

"Remember to keep holy the Sabbath day." Do you intentionally miss Mass or holy days of obligation? Do you set aside necessary time on Sundays to rest and visit with family? Do you show reverence to God when you are in his house?

### Fourth Commandment

"Honor your father and your mother." Do you disobey or disrespect your parents or other superiors? Do you neglect your responsibilities to your parents? Do you show your thanks and appreciation to your parents for all they do?

### Fifth Commandment

"You shall not kill." Have you physically injured another person? Do you get angry or act maliciously toward others? Have you ever used alcohol or drugs or cut yourself? Have you ever participated in an abortion either directly or indirectly?

### Sixth and Ninth Commandments

"You shall not commit adultery." "You shall not covet your neighbor's wife." Do you willingly entertain impure thoughts or desires? Do you use impure or suggestive language? Have you ever bought or viewed pornography? Have you ever committed impure acts with another or with yourself?

### Eighth Commandment

"You shall not bear false witness against your neighbor." Do you intentionally lie? Do you deceive others or spread gossip? Do you fail to keep confidential information?

### Seventh and Tenth Commandments

"You shall not steal." "You shall not covet your neighbor's goods." Have you ever stolen, cheated, or encouraged another to steal or cheat? Are you envious of other peoples' goods? Do you make getting material possessions the purpose of your life?

### Act of Contrition

My God, I am sorry for my sins with all my heart. In choosing to do wrong and failing to do good, I have sinned against you whom I should love above all things. I firmly intend, with your help, to do penance, to sin no more, and to avoid whatever leads me to sin. Our Savior Jesus Christ suffered and died for us. In his name, my God, have mercy. Amen.

# Notes

For use with Rosary activity at end of Session Seven (page 28).

These two pages are available as a free download from BibleStudyforCatholics.com.

38 **ENCOUNTER** experiencing God in the everyday

## HOW TO PRAY THE ROSARY

The Rosary is a prayer directed to Jesus, through and with his Mother, Mary. The guided, scriptural prayers that we pray on the beads (the Our Father, Hail Mary, and Glory Be) help us pray. They are especially useful when your mind or body are tired or you can't seem to "find the right words" to pray. And remember that we must always keep in mind Jesus' warning not to let our prayers become repetitious babbling or empty phrases (Mt. 6:7).

Sometimes it helps to recite the prayers more slowly, to ensure we are *praying* and not just *saying* the prayers. So, grab your rosary beads and give it a try! Maybe start with just one decade and build from there. And as you begin, ask Mary to kneel beside you and pray with you—you'll be amazed at how much your relationship with Jesus grows through this awesome Catholic prayer.

1.  **Make the Sign of the Cross**
2.  **Pray the Apostles Creed -** Crucifix

    *I believe in God, the Father Almighty, Creator of heaven and earth, and in Jesus Christ, his only Son, our Lord, who was conceived by the Holy Spirit, born of the Virgin Mary, suffered under Pontius Pilate, was crucified, died and was buried; he descended into hell; on the third day he rose again from the dead; he ascended into heaven, and is seated at the right hand of God, the Father Almighty; from there he will come to judge the living and the dead. I believe in the Holy Spirit, the holy catholic Church, the communion of saints, the forgiveness of sins, the resurrection of the body, and life everlasting. Amen.*

3.  **Pray an Our Father –** 1st bead

    *Our Father, who art in heaven, hallowed be thy name; thy kingdom come; thy will be done on earth as it is in heaven. Give us this day our daily bread; and forgive us our trespasses as we forgive those who trespass against us; and lead us not into temptation, but deliver us from evil. Amen.*

4.  **Pray three Hail Marys –** 2nd through 4th beads

    *Hail Mary, full of grace, the Lord is with you; blessed are you among women, and blessed is the fruit of your womb, Jesus. Holy Mary, Mother of God, pray for us sinners now and at the hour of our death. Amen.*

5.  **Pray a Glory Be and the (optional) Fatima Prayer –** 5th bead

    *Glory be to the Father, the Son, and the Holy Spirit; as it was in the beginning, is now, and ever shall be, world without end. Amen.*

    *O my Jesus, forgive us our sins, save us from the fires of hell, lead all souls to heaven, especially those in most need of thy mercy.*

6.  **Announce the first mystery, then pray the Our Father.**
7.  **Pray ten Hail Marys while meditating on the mystery on the next ten beads (a "decade").**
8.  **When you get to the next single bead, pray the Glory Be and the (optional) Fatima Prayer. Announce the second mystery while on the same bead.**
9.  **Repeat steps 6-8 for each of the three remaining mysteries.**
10. **After you've finished the fifth mystery and are back to the center piece, finish the Rosary by praying the Hail Holy Queen …**

**Notes**

*Hail, holy Queen, mother of mercy, our life, our sweetness, and our hope. To you we cry, poor banished children of Eve; to you we send up our sighs, mourning and weeping in this valley of tears.*

*Turn, then, most gracious advocate, your eyes of mercy toward us; and after this, our exile, show unto us the blessed fruit of your womb, Jesus. O clement, O loving, O sweet Virgin Mary.*

**Leader:** *Pray for us, O Holy Mother of God …*

**All:** *That we may be made worthy of the promises of Christ.*

**Leader:** *Let us pray.*

**All:** *O God, whose only begotten Son, by his life, death, and resurrection, has purchased for us the rewards of eternal life; grant, we beseech thee, that meditating upon these mysteries of the Most Holy Rosary of the Blessed Virgin Mary, we may imitate what they contain and obtain what they promise, through the same Christ our Lord. Amen.*

**Joyful Mysteries** (Monday, Saturday)
The Annunciation: Luke 1:26-33, 38
The Visitation: Luke 1:39-45
The Nativity of Jesus: Luke 2:6-12
The Presentation of Jesus: Luke 2:25-32
The Finding of Jesus: Luke 2:41-50

**Sorrowful Mysteries** (Tuesday, Friday)
The Agony in the Garden: Luke 22:39-46
The Scourging at the Pillar: Mark 15:6-15
The Crowning with Thorns: John 19:1-8
The Carrying of the Cross: John 19:16-22
The Crucifixion: John 19:25-30

**Glorious Mysteries** ( Wednesday, Sunday)
The Resurrection: Mark 16:1-7
The Ascension of Jesus: Luke 24:45-53
The Descent of the Holy Spirit: Acts 2:1-7, 11
The Assumption of Mary: Luke 1:46-55
The Coronation of Mary: Revelation 12:1-7

**Luminous Mysteries** (Thursday)
The Baptism of Jesus: Matthew 3:13-17
The Miracle at Cana: John 2:1-11
The Proclamation of the Kingdom: Mark 1:14-15
The Transfiguration: Matthew 17:1-8
The Institution of the Eucharist: Matthew 26:26-28

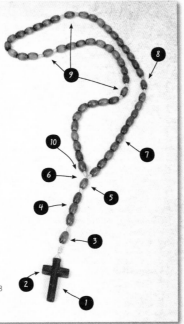

*It might be difficult for you to pray the Rosary at first. I'll be honest with you—even though I pray it daily, it can still be tough because the soothing repetition can almost put you to sleep sometimes. The rhythm can be both a good thing and a bad thing (if you're like me). I have to work very hard to stay focused. Kneeling helps.*

# Notes

40 **ENCOUNTER** experiencing God in the everyday

# Continuing Your Journey

## GREAT VERSES FOR YOUNG MEN

"Likewise urge the younger men to control themselves. Show yourself in all respects a model of good deeds, and in your teaching show integrity, gravity, and sound speech that cannot be censured, so that an opponent may be put to shame, having nothing evil to say of us" **(Titus 2:6-8).**

"Do your best to present yourself to God as one approved, a workman who has no need to be ashamed, rightly handling the word of truth" **(2 Timothy 2:15).**

"Let no evil talk come out of your mouths, but only such as is good for edifying, as fits the occasion, that it may impart grace to those who hear" **(Ephesians 4:29).**

"But I am afraid that as the serpent deceived Eve by his cunning, your thoughts will be led astray from a sincere and pure devotion to Christ" **(2 Corinthians 11:3).**

"I appeal to you therefore, brethren, by the mercies of God, to present your bodies as a living sacrifice, holy and acceptable to God, which is your spiritual worship. Do not be conformed to this world but be transformed by the renewal of your mind, that you may prove what is the will of God, what is good and acceptable and perfect" **(Romans 12:1-2).**

"For all that is in the world, the lust of the flesh and the lust of the eyes and the pride of life, is not of the Father but is of the world. And the world passes away, and the lust of it; but he who does the will of God abides for ever" **(1 John 2:16-17).**

"Finally, brethren, whatever is true, whatever is honorable, whatever is just, whatever is pure, whatever is lovely, whatever is gracious, if there is any excellence, if there is anything worthy of praise, think about these things" **(Philippians 4:8).**

---

Encourage your students to keep these "Great Verses" in their Bibles or to hang them in their bedrooms, to read them often, and to commit them to memory. They are available as a free download from BibleStudyforCatholics.com.

## Notes

Continuing Your Journey    41

# GREAT VERSES
# FOR YOUNG WOMEN

"Charm is deceitful, and beauty is vain, but a woman who fears the Lord is to be praised" **(Proverbs 31:30).**

"Therefore encourage one another and build one another up, just as you are doing" **(1 Thessalonians 5:11).**

"Know this, my beloved brethren. Let every man be quick to hear, slow to speak, slow to anger, for the anger of man does not work the righteousness of God" **(James 1:19-20).**

"Let not yours be the outward adorning with braiding of hair, decoration of gold, and wearing of robes, but let it be the hidden person of the heart with the imperishable jewel of a gentle and quiet spirit, which in God's sight is very precious" **(1 Peter 3:3-4).**

"Not that I complain of want; for I have learned, in whatever state I am, to be content" **(Philippians 4:11).**

"Shun immorality. Every other sin which a man commits is outside the body; but the immoral man sins against his own body. Do you not know that your body is a temple of the Holy Spirit within you, which you have from God? You are not your own; you were bought with a price. So glorify God in your body" **(1 Corinthians 6:18-20).**

"For this is the will of God, your sanctification: that you abstain from immorality. … For God has not called us for uncleanness, but in holiness. Therefore whoever disregards this, disregards not man but God, who gives his Holy Spirit to you" **(1 Thessalonians 4:3, 7-8).**

"For I know the plans I have for you, says the Lord, plans for welfare and not for evil, to give you a future and a hope" **(Jeremiah 29:11).**

These verses are perfect to use with *lectio divina*. (pages 32-33)

**Notes**

42 **ENCOUNTER** experiencing God in the everyday

## THE WORD FOR THE DAY

Living the Catholic life isn't easy. Being a Christian in today's world requires a lot of patience with challenging people and constant prayer for people, especially those within your own family. Below is a list of different emotions, feelings, struggles, or challenges that you will face on a daily or weekly basis, as well as a passage from the Bible that might offer you some hope, direction, and insight. Happy reading!

Worried about what your future holds? **Jeremiah 29:11**

Can't find the "right words" when you pray? **Matthew 6:9-15**

Feeling like no one will listen to you because you're too young? **1 Timothy 4:12**

Down on yourself because you keep messing up? **Romans 3:23**

Concerned that God has "abandoned" you? **Matthew 28:20**

Are you afraid to confess your sins? **1 John 1:9**

What should you do about your "enemies"? **Luke 6:35**

Need confidence before you start your day? **Psalms 62:1-2**

Nothing you do ... nothing, can make God love you less. **Romans 8:38-39**

Are you tired of "doing the right thing"? **2 Thessalonians 3:13**

Are you overwhelmed by temptation? **1 Corinthians 10:13**

Want to know the secret to being "great" in God's eyes? **Luke 22:26**

Feeling tired or weak? **Isaiah 40:28-31**

Feeling alone or down? **Joshua 1:9**

Do you ever feel like just "losing it" with someone? **Proverbs 13:3-4**

Why be holy? **1 Peter 1:15-16**

Ever wonder if God is really listening to your prayers? **Jeremiah 29:12**

Have you been hurt by others' actions? **2 Corinthians 12:20**

Are you afraid to trust God with your whole life? **Romans 9:33**

Is remaining pure a struggle for you or your friends? **1 Thessalonians 4:7**

Have you "given up" on certain friends or family ever following God? **Matthew 19:26**

## The Word for the Day

This handy resource provides relevant, timely suggestions for those looking for answers to life's daily dilemmas. Not only is this "extra" a valuable guide to the youth, but it's a worthwhile tool for any catechists who find themselves put on the spot. It offers them a hopeful word or counsel.

Encourage your students to keep this list handy, and encourage leaders to commit as many of these passages as they can to memory. You never know when the Holy Spirit is going to call upon that knowledge!

 AWFUL BIBLE JOKES

Q: What kind of man was Boaz before he got married?
*A: Ruth-less.*

Q: At what time of day was Adam created?
*A: A little before Eve.*

Q: Where was the first math problem mentioned in the Bible?
*A: In Genesis, when God told Adam and Eve to go forth and multiply.*

Q: On the ark, Noah probably got milk from the cows onboard. What did he get from the ducks?
*A: Quackers.*

Q: Which animal on Noah's ark had the highest level of intelligence?
*A: The giraffe.*

Q: When was the first lunch meat mentioned in the Bible?
*A: When Noah took Ham into the ark.*

Q: How many people went on board the ark before Noah?
*A: Three, because it says "Noah went forth" (Genesis 8:18).*

Q: Why was everyone in biblical times so poor?
*A: Because there was only one Job.*

Q: How long did Cain dislike his brother?
*A: As long as he was Abel.*

Q: What was Noah's greatest worry?
*A: The pair of termites.*

Q: Who was the greatest comedian in the Bible?
*A: Samson. He brought the house down.*

Q: Why couldn't Noah's wife and sons play cards on the ark?
*A: Because Noah sat on the deck.*

Q: The ark was built in three stories, and the top story had a window to let light in, but how did they get light to the bottom two stories?
*A: They used floodlights.*

Q: What do they call pastors in Germany?
*A: German Shepherds.*

Q: Who was the most flagrant lawbreaker in the Bible?
*A: Moses. Because he broke all ten commandments at once.*

Q: Which Bible character had no parents?
*A: Joshua, son of Nun.*

Q: Where was Solomon's temple located?
*A: On the side of his head.*

Q: Which Old Testament character was known for having a foul mouth at a young age?
*A: Job—he cursed the day he was born (Job 3:1).*

Q: What do you call a sleepwalking nun?
*A: A roamin' Catholic!*

Keep these jokes and the "Brain Teasers" and "Did You Know" questions (on pages 46-47) handy to keep the kids' attention or to fill time as needed.

**Notes**

Use these extra activities to fill time in class, or let the kids do them at home.

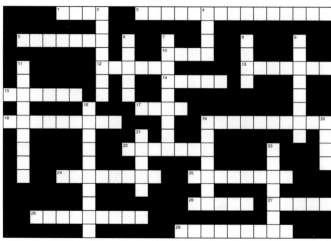

44 **ENCOUNTER** experiencing God in the everyday

## HOW WELL DO YOU KNOW THE BIBLE?

**Across**

1. What did Jesus give Peter to represent his papal authority?
3. When did three apostles see Jesus with Moses and Elijah?
5. What archangel fought the devil in Revelation 12?
10. What was Mary's mother's name?
12. The Greek word for "witness" is _____.
13. Who did Jesus raise from the dead after four days?
14. What did Jesus change Simon's name to?
15. She was Moses' sister.
17. Where did Jesus perform his first miracle?
18. This man climbed a tree to get a better view of Jesus.
19. What was the name of the garden where Jesus was arrested?
22. Who told Mary she would conceive a son?
24. What was the name of the apostle who succeeded Judas?
25. Where did Jesus grow up?
26. How many sons did Noah have?
27. This king sought to kill the baby Jesus.
28. On what feast did the Holy Spirit descend upon the apostles?
29. Christ quoted this psalm from the cross.

**Down**

2. What king followed King David?
4. How many loaves of bread did Jesus multiply?
6. He was Moses' brother.
7. Jesus worked as a _____.
8. What river did God turn to blood (in Exodus 7)?
9. What was the name of the criminal Pilate released in Jesus' place?
11. Who was Mary's cousin, the mother of John the Baptist?
16. This list begins: "Blessed are the poor …"
19. Who did David fight with a slingshot?
20. What was the name of the garden where Adam and Eve lived?
21. What was the name of Abraham's wife?
23. Which apostle was a tax collector?

Answers on page 48

**Notes**

## WHO'S WHO IN THE BIBLE?

**Across**

1. This prophet was a young man when God called him.
3. He was Eve's third son.
7. Who was swallowed by a large fish?
8. Moses' wife's name was _____.
10. He was Eve's husband.
11. Adam's wife was _____.
13. Moses' brother's name was _____.
14. Who "took over" after Moses?
15. This king sought to kill the baby Jesus.
17. What Philistine warrior battled David?
21. He was released (by Pilate) instead of Jesus.
22. What queen saved her people?
23. God warned him about the Flood.
25. What shepherd slayed the giant?
31. This angel battled the devil.
32. She is the first prophetess mentioned in the New Testament.
33. His name means "laughter."
34. Jesus raised this good friend from the dead.
35. He married the widow, Ruth.
36. This cousin of Mary proclaimed her "Blessed …"

**Down**

2. Moses' sister's name was _____.
4. Paul wrote to this young bishop.
5. Who is the Bible's "strongest man"?
6. He was Eve's first son.
7. Moses' father-in-law was named _____.
9. God changed Jacob's name to _____.
11. This prophet took on the "prophets" of Baal.
12. He was Mark's cousin and traveled with Paul.
16. This angel visited Mary.
18. Her son, Samuel, became a mighty prophet.
19. This apostle also went by the name Jude.
20. She was the wife of David and the mother of Solomon.
24. She was Isaac's wife and Leah's little sister.
26. This prophet's book is the longest.
27. This leader "washed his hands" of Jesus.
28. St. Paul was first known as _____.
29. She saved her family's lives in Jericho.
30. She was Abraham's wife.

Answers on page 48

---

# Notes

46 **ENCOUNTER** experiencing God in the everyday

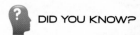 **DID YOU KNOW?**

1.  Israelites were forbidden (in Old Testament times) to wear clothes made of two kinds of material. So much for 50 percent cotton and 50 percent polyester!

2.  The word "manna" literally means, "What is it?"

3.  There weren't just two of every animal on the ark. In fact, there were seven pairs of all the clean animals (Genesis 7:2-4).

4.  In 2 Samuel 21:20-21, it says that Jonathan killed a man who had six fingers on each hand and six toes on each foot. Seriously.

5.  King David had twenty children (1 Chronicles 3:1-9). They probably didn't go out to eat very much.

6.  Abraham was 100 years old when his son, Isaac, was born (Genesis 21:5). Imagine him trying to keep up at the playground.

7.  St. Paul and the early Christian disciples would pray every day at 3 PM (Acts 3:1). Many people still do it.

8.  King Solomon had 12,000 horses (1 Kings 10:26). Imagine the smell.

9.  King Solomon imported peacocks to decorate his palace (1 Kings 10:22). Throw pillows probably would have been less messy.

10. Job had 3,000 camels (Job 1:3) … animals, not cigarettes.

11. St. Paul was in a shipwreck on a boat with 276 people on board (Acts 27:37). In fact, Paul was shipwrecked three different times.

12. The Garden of Eden had four different rivers: Pishon, Gihon, Tigris, and Euphrates (Genesis 2:11-14). Any of those sound familiar from social studies?

**Notes**

 **BRAIN TEASERS**

1. After a prank went wrong, a student was told, "If you tell a lie, you will get suspended; if you tell the truth, you will still get a detention." What could he say to avoid both?

2. How far can Jesus travel into the desert?

3. What do these three sentences have in common that is usually uncommon?
   - Saints don't punch animals.
   - A saint is a good Catholic.
   - It is unusual to think of a story about a Catholic saint who ran into a volcano.

4. What was given to you that others use more than you do, but that can't get used up?

5. What binds two people, is used by one, and is seen by all?

6. Speak its name aloud and it disappears. What is it?

7. Remove three letters from this sequence to reveal a famous saint: THAREUEGLUESTTTIERNSE

8. Sister Teresa bets Sister Mary that whatever Sister Mary can pull in a wagon halfway up a hill, she can pull all the way up the hill. How can Sister Mary win the bet?

9. How can you spell reconciliation using only five different letters?

10. What does a priest change daily, yet never looks different?

Answers on page 49

## Catholic Brain Teasers – Answers

1. *"You will suspend me."*

2. *Halfway. After that, he will be traveling out of the desert.*

3. *They don't have any "E's" in them.*

4. *Your name.*

5. *Wedding ring.*

6. *Silence.*

7. *Augustine (remove THREE LETTERS).*

8. *Pull Sister Teresa in the wagon.*

9. *Mercy.*

10. *Bread and wine.*

48 **ENCOUNTER** experiencing God in the everyday

# Answer Key

### HOW WELL DO YOU KNOW THE BIBLE? (FROM PAGE 44)

### WHO'S WHO IN THE BIBLE? (FROM PAGE 45)

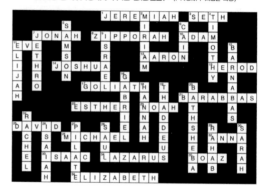

**Notes**

## BRAIN TEASERS - ANSWERS (FROM PAGE 47)

1. *"You will suspend me."*

2. *Halfway. After that, he will be traveling out of the desert.*

3. *They don't have any "E's" in them.*

4. *Your name.*

5. *Wedding ring.*

6. *Silence.*

7. *Augustine (remove THREE LETTERS).*

8. *Pull Sister Teresa in the wagon.*

9. *Mercy.*

10. *Bread and wine.*

## THE DIVINE DESIGNER ENDNOTES (FROM PAGE 8)

1 CK-12 Foundation, *CK-12.org,* ck12.org/book/CK-12-Biology-Concepts/r11/, October 16, 2012.

2 Charles Q. Choi and Jeanna Bryner, Ed., "Brute Force: Humans Can Sure Take a Punch," *LiveScience,* livescience.com/6040-brute-force-humans-punch.html, October 16, 2012.

3 Ed Grabianowski, "How many skin cells do you shed every day?" *HowStuffWorks.com, Discovery Fit and Health,* health.howstuffworks.com/skin-care/information/anatomy/shed-skin-cells.html, October 17, 2012.

4 Georgia State University, *HyperPhysics,* hyperphysics.phy-astr.gsu.edu/hbase/vision/rodcone.html, October 16, 2012.

5 Sue Caldwell, "Renal (Kidney) Physiology," Grossmont College, grossmont.edu/suecaldwell/141_excretory.htm, 2012.

6 Vogt, "Introduction to Astronomy: The Tilt of the Earth," New Mexico State University, web.nmsu.edu/~esgerken/lecture07/slide04.html, 2009.

7 The Library of Congress, *Library of Congress Online,* loc.gov/rr/scitech/mysteries/snowcrystals.html, October 17, 2012.

8 David Wallechinsky and Amy Wallace, *The People's Almanac* (Melbourne, New York: CANONGATE, 1986).

9 W.C. Lindemann and C.R. Glover, "Nitrogen Fixation by Legumes," New Mexico State University and the US Department of Agriculture, May 2003.

10 United States Department of Commerce, *National Ocean Service,* oceanservice.noaa.gov/facts/oceandepth.html, October 16, 2012.

11 Fraser Cain, "What Percentage of the Earth's Land Surface is Desert?" *Universe Today,* universetoday.com/65639/what-percentage-of-the-earths-land-surface-is-desert/, June 1, 2010.

12 US Geological Survey, The USGS Water Science School, ga.water.usgs.gov/edu/earthhowmuch.html, October 16, 2012.

13 Nicholos Wethington, "How many stars are in the Milky Way," *Universe Today,* universetoday.com/22380/how-many-stars-are-in-the-milky-way/, December 16, 2008.

**Notes**